DAILY DOSE
of
KNOWLEDGE™

BRILLIANT
THOUGHTS

WEST
SIDE
PUBLISHING

Scripture quotations marked (KJV) are taken from the HOLY BIBLE, KING JAMES VERSION.

Scripture quotations marked (NIV) are taken from the HOLY BIBLE, NEW INTERNATIONAL VERSION®. NIV®. Copyright© 1973, 1978, 1984 by International Bible Society. Used by permission of Zondervan. All rights reserved.

Cover photos: **Getty Images** (center & right); **Kansas State Historical Society, Topeka/Kean Archives** (left)

Daily Dose of Knowledge is a trademark of West Side Publishing.

West Side Publishing is a division of Publications International, Ltd.

Louis Weber, CEO
Publications International, Ltd.
7373 North Cicero Avenue
Lincolnwood, Illinois 60712

Permission is never granted for commercial purposes.

ISBN-13: 978-1-4127-1585-0
ISBN-10: 1-4127-1585-7

Manufactured in China.

8 7 6 5 4 3 2 1

Library of Congress Control Number: 2008928348

ALL WORDS are pegs
to hang ideas on.

Henry Ward Beecher

A Collection of Brilliant Thoughts

According to author Toni Morrison, language acts as a measure of life. The novelist Thomas Mann described speech as "civilization itself." And the dramatist Johann Wolfgang von Goethe suggested that when ideas fail, words come to the rescue. There's a common thread among these various observations: that language significantly shapes the human experience.

Words seep into every corner of our daily lives: the conversations we have, the books we read, the stories we hear on the news, and the e-mails we write. Words inform and transform our experiences; they define and enrich our interactions. Our purpose in making this book is to enable you to encounter words used wisely and used well. Our aim is that you might discover, on a daily basis, brilliant words that make you think.

Daily Dose of Knowledge^{TM}: *Brilliant Thoughts* captures our timeless love of words and enduring fascination with carefully crafted language. Containing hundreds of quotations from a wide range of people, this book collects profound, humorous, thought-provoking, witty, memorable, playful, and (we think) brilliant words. You'll recognize thoughts from notable, widely quoted people (Abraham Lincoln, Mark Twain, Helen Keller, Martin Luther King, Jr.), as well as plenty of quotes from lesser known but nonetheless brilliant thinkers (Annie Dillard, Pierre Teilhard de Chardin, Wendell Berry, and Ursula K. Le Guin). There are quotes addressing aging, ambition, imagination, and perseverance, and statements about money, justice, politics, and power. Some quotes are lighthearted comments by such comedic talents as Jerry Seinfeld, Phyllis Diller, Jon Stewart, and Lily Tomlin. Others are contemplative thoughts by religious figures, scholars, and saints, such as Buddha, Jesus, Søren Kierkegaard, and St. Augustine. There are quotes by artists, writers, and musicians addressing the creative process, as well as remarks by scientists, economists, and politicians on past lessons, present conditions, and the future of the planet.

In other words, this book has something for everyone. *Daily Dose of Knowledge*[TM]: *Brilliant Thoughts* is uniquely structured so that each day of the year you receive a palatable dose of information and insight. It is organized by week, and each page contains a range of quotes from different people on different subjects. Whereas other quotation collections are often organized by subject or attribution, this book mixes together subjects and sources to allow for what we hope is a more compelling, enlightening, and varied reading experience. Just as our days are filled with various types of language, from jokes to serious conversations, so too are the pages of *Daily Dose of Knowledge*[TM]: *Brilliant Thoughts* filled with different types of quotations, with Woody Allen's one-liners and Emily Dickinson's poetic insights occupying the same page. In case you'd like to find all of the quotes by a certain person or about a certain subject, we've indexed the information by source and subject to allow for quick reference.

We sincerely hope that you enjoy this collection and that it not only exposes you to a variety of brilliant thoughts but also provides you with a daily dose of knowledge and inspiration.

MAN CANNOT DISCOVER new oceans unless he has the courage to lose sight of the shore.

André Gide

❧ ❧ ❧ ❧

AS WE ACQUIRE more knowledge, things do not become more comprehensible, but more mysterious.

Dr. Albert Schweitzer

❧ ❧ ❧ ❧

NOT ONLY IS THE universe stranger than we think, it is stranger than we can think.

Werner Heisenberg

❧ ❧ ❧ ❧

SOME PEOPLE NEVER go crazy. What truly horrible lives they must lead.

Charles Bukowski

❧ ❧ ❧ ❧

HUMANKIND HAS NOT woven the web of life. We are but one thread within it. Whatever we do to the web, we do to ourselves. All things are bound together. All things connect.

Chief Seattle

❧ ❧ ❧ ❧

THERE ARE PEOPLE who want to be everywhere at once, and they get nowhere.

Carl Sandburg

❧ ❧ ❧ ❧

MAN IS BORN to live, not to prepare for life.

Boris Pasternak

⚜ ⚜ ⚜ ⚜

WE MAKE A LIVING by what we get, we make a life by what we give.

Winston Churchill

⚜ ⚜ ⚜ ⚜

TO ACHIEVE THE MARVELOUS, it is precisely the unthinkable that must be thought.

Tom Robbins

⚜ ⚜ ⚜ ⚜

YOU WILL FIND something more in woods than in books. Trees and stones will teach you that which you can never learn from masters.

St. Bernard of Clairvaux

⚜ ⚜ ⚜ ⚜

THE RIPEST PEACH is highest on the tree.

James Whitcomb Riley

⚜ ⚜ ⚜ ⚜

I REALIZED THAT if I was going to achieve anything in life I had to be aggressive. I had to get out there and go for it . . . . I know fear is an obstacle for some people, but it's an illusion to me.

Michael Jordan

⚜ ⚜ ⚜ ⚜

WE'D ALL LIKE a reputation for generosity, and we'd all like to buy it cheap.

Mignon McLaughlin

⚜ ⚜ ⚜ ⚜

TO LIVE IS SO STARTLING it leaves but little room for other occupations.

Emily Dickinson

⚜ ⚜ ⚜ ⚜

LIFE IS WHAT we make it. Always has been, always will be.

Grandma Moses

⚜ ⚜ ⚜ ⚜

THE SKY ABOVE the port was the color of television, tuned to a dead channel.

William Gibson

⚜ ⚜ ⚜ ⚜

I ACCEPT CHAOS. I am not sure whether it accepts me. I know some people are terrified of the bomb. But there are other people terrified to be seen carrying a modern screen magazine. Experience teaches us that silence terrifies people the most.

Bob Dylan

⚜ ⚜ ⚜ ⚜

MY ONE REGRET in life is that I'm not someone else.

Woody Allen

⚜ ⚜ ⚜ ⚜

IF YOU HAVE MADE mistakes, even serious ones, there is always another chance for you. What we call failure is not the falling down, but the staying down.

Mary Pickford

❧ ❧ ❧ ❧

TECHNOLOGY: THE KNACK of so arranging the world that we need not experience it.

Max Frisch

❧ ❧ ❧ ❧

LOVE SHOULD BE SIMPLE, but it's not. Hate should be hard, but it's easy.

Tanya Tucker

❧ ❧ ❧ ❧

MAN, AS WE KNOW HIM, is a poor creature, but he is halfway between an ape and a god and he is traveling in the right direction.

Dean Inge

❧ ❧ ❧ ❧

I CAN'T UNDERSTAND why people are frightened of new ideas. I'm frightened of the old ones.

John Cage

❧ ❧ ❧ ❧

CONSISTENCY IS the last refuge of the unimaginative.

Oscar Wilde

❧ ❧ ❧ ❧

IF WE LISTENED to our intellect, we'd never have a love affair. We'd never have a friendship. We'd never go into business, because we'd be too cynical. Well, that's nonsense. You've got to jump off cliffs all the time and build your wings on the way down.

Annie Dillard

❖ ❖ ❖ ❖

BEER IS PROOF that God loves us and wants us to be happy.

Benjamin Franklin

❖ ❖ ❖ ❖

OPPORTUNITIES multiply as they are seized.

Sun Tzu

❖ ❖ ❖ ❖

WE SHOULDN'T TEACH great books; we should teach love of reading.

B. F. Skinner

❖ ❖ ❖ ❖

THERE IS NO CURE for birth and death save to enjoy the interval.

George Santayana

❖ ❖ ❖ ❖

HE WAS DULL in a new way, and that made many people think him great.

Samuel Johnson

❖ ❖ ❖ ❖

IT IS THROUGH generating stories of our own crisis and hope and telling them to one another that we light the path.

Rosemary Radford Reuther

❧ ❧ ❧ ❧

AGE IS A QUESTION of mind over matter. If you don't mind, it doesn't matter.

Satchel Paige

❧ ❧ ❧ ❧

IF YOU TALK to God, you are praying; if God talks to you, you have schizophrenia.

Thomas Szasz

❧ ❧ ❧ ❧

SHOW ME A HERO and I will write you a tragedy.

F. Scott Fitzgerald

❧ ❧ ❧ ❧

SUFFERING is overrated.

Bill Veeck

❧ ❧ ❧ ❧

THE DAY WILL come when, after harnessing space, the winds, the tides, gravitation, we shall harness for God the energies of love. And, on that day, for the second time in the history of the world, man will have discovered fire.

Pierre Teilhard de Chardin

❧ ❧ ❧ ❧

SILENCE IS ARGUMENT carried on by other means.

Ernesto "Che" Guevara

�֍ ✤ ✤ ✤

LIFE IS PLEASANT. Death is peaceful. It's the transition that's troublesome.

Isaac Asimov

✤ ✤ ✤ ✤

I UNDERSTAND WHY the saints were rarely married women. I am convinced it has nothing inherently to do, as I once supposed, with chastity or children. It has to do primarily with distractions.... Women's normal occupations in general run counter to creative life, or contemplative life, or saintly life.

Anne Morrow Lindbergh

✤ ✤ ✤ ✤

WE ARE BORN princes and the civilizing process makes us frogs.

Eric Berne

✤ ✤ ✤ ✤

ANXIETY is the dizziness of freedom.

Søren Kierkegaard

✤ ✤ ✤ ✤

IF YOU TELL the truth about how you're feeling, it becomes funny.

Larry David

✤ ✤ ✤ ✤

IT IS THAT WILLING SUSPENSION of disbelief for the moment, which constitutes poetic faith.

Samuel Taylor Coleridge

⚜ ⚜ ⚜ ⚜

TWO THINGS FILL the mind with ever new and increasing admiration and awe, the more often and more enduringly reflection is occupied with them: the starry heavens above me and the moral law within me.

Immanuel Kant

⚜ ⚜ ⚜ ⚜

I WANT TO be all used up when I die.

George Bernard Shaw

⚜ ⚜ ⚜ ⚜

LIFE ITSELF is the proper binge.

Julia Child

⚜ ⚜ ⚜ ⚜

CLOTHES MAKE the man. Naked people have little or no influence in society.

Mark Twain

⚜ ⚜ ⚜ ⚜

JUST BECAUSE something doesn't do what you planned it to do doesn't mean it's useless.

Thomas Alva Edison

⚜ ⚜ ⚜ ⚜

I SEE NO OBJECTION to stoutness, in moderation.

W. S. Gilbert

WHEN PEOPLE TELL you how young you look, they are also telling you how old you are.

Cary Grant

FINANCE IS THE ART of passing currency from hand to hand until it finally disappears.

Robert W. Sarnoff

BUT, GENTLEMEN, enough of words. Actions speak louder than. Action now.

Anthony Burgess

I'M LOOKING FORWARD to the most fascinating experience in life, which is dying. You've got to approach your dying the way you live your life—with curiosity, with hope, with fascination, and with courage.

Timothy Leary

LIFE IS SOMETHING to do when you can't get to sleep.

Fran Lebowitz

NEUROSIS IS THE WAY of avoiding nonbeing by avoiding being.

Paul Tillich

❦ ❦ ❦ ❦

IT IS WELL TO REMEMBER that the entire population of the universe, with one trifling exception, is composed of others.

John Andrew Holmes

❦ ❦ ❦ ❦

VIRTUE HAS its own reward, but no sale at the box office.

Mae West

❦ ❦ ❦ ❦

A REAL FRIEND is one who walks in when the rest of the world walks out.

Walter Winchell

❦ ❦ ❦ ❦

THE STRONGEST MAN in the world is he who stands most alone.

Henrik Ibsen

❦ ❦ ❦ ❦

SOME PEOPLE SWALLOW the universe like a pill; they travel on through the world, like smiling images pushed from behind. For God's sake, give me the young man who has brains enough to make a fool of himself!

Robert Louis Stevenson

❦ ❦ ❦ ❦

LIVING IS A FORM of not being sure, not knowing what next or how. The moment you know how, you begin to die a little. The artist never entirely knows. We guess. We may be wrong, but we take leap after leap in the dark.

Agnes DeMille

⚜ ⚜ ⚜ ⚜

THE ONLY ZEN you find on the tops of mountains is the Zen you bring up there.

Robert M. Pirsig

⚜ ⚜ ⚜ ⚜

A SOCIETY BASED on cash and self-interest is not a society at all, but a state of war.

William Morris

⚜ ⚜ ⚜ ⚜

REMINISCENCES make one feel so deliciously aged and sad.

George Bernard Shaw

⚜ ⚜ ⚜ ⚜

ALL LIFE is a dream, and dreams are dreams.

Pedro Calderón de la Barca

⚜ ⚜ ⚜ ⚜

I THINK YOUR whole life shows in your face, and you should be proud of that.

Lauren Bacall

⚜ ⚜ ⚜ ⚜

NO JUSTICE, no peace.

Sonny Carson

❖ ❖ ❖ ❖

I HAVE NO RIGHT, by anything I do or say, to demean a human being in his own eyes. What matters is not what I think of him; it is what he thinks of himself. To undermine a man's self-respect is a sin.

Antoine de Saint-Exupéry

❖ ❖ ❖ ❖

A SHIP IN HARBOR is safe, but that is not what ships are built for.

John A. Shedd

❖ ❖ ❖ ❖

YOU CAN'T WAKE a person who is pretending to be asleep.

Navajo proverb

❖ ❖ ❖ ❖

WITHOUT A HINT of irony I can say I have been blessed with brilliant enemies. . . . I owe them a great debt, because they redoubled my energies and drove me in new directions.

Edward O. Wilson

❖ ❖ ❖ ❖

THERE'S ALWAYS something suspect about an intellectual on the winning side.

Václav Havel

❖ ❖ ❖ ❖

WE DIDN'T LOSE the game; we just ran out of time.

Vince Lombardi

⚜ ⚜ ⚜ ⚜

TO KNOW ALL IS not to forgive all. It is to despise everybody.

Quentin Crisp

⚜ ⚜ ⚜ ⚜

THERE ARE TIMES I think I am not sure of something which I absolutely know.

Mongkut, King of Siam

⚜ ⚜ ⚜ ⚜

TIME TICKS BY; we grow older. Before we know it, too much has passed and we've missed the chance to have had other people hurt us. To a younger me this sounded like luck; to an older me this sounds like a quiet tragedy.

Douglas Coupland

⚜ ⚜ ⚜ ⚜

LET THERE BE spaces in your togetherness.

Kahlil Gibran

⚜ ⚜ ⚜ ⚜

THE HAPPINESS OF LIFE, on the contrary, is made up of minute fractions—the little, soon-forgotten charities of a kiss, a smile, a kind look, a heartfelt compliment . . . and the countless infinitesimals of pleasurable and genial feeling.

Samuel Taylor Coleridge

⚜ ⚜ ⚜ ⚜

EVERYWHERE ONE seeks to produce meaning, to make the world signify, to render it visible. We are not, however, in danger of lacking meaning; quite the contrary, we are gorged with meaning and it is killing us.

Jean Baudrillard

✤ ✤ ✤ ✤

CLOUDS NOW and again
Give a soul some respite from
Moon-gazing—behold.

Matsuo Basho

✤ ✤ ✤ ✤

THE WILLINGNESS to accept responsibility for one's life is the source from which self-respect springs.

Joan Didion

✤ ✤ ✤ ✤

WHEN ONE'S expectations are reduced to zero, one really appreciates everything that one does have.

Stephen Hawking

✤ ✤ ✤ ✤

THE WORLD will be saved by beauty.

Fyodor Dostoyevsky

✤ ✤ ✤ ✤

WE MUST NOT confuse dissent with disloyalty.

Edward R. Murrow

✤ ✤ ✤ ✤

BUT IN TRUTH there are only three types of people in the world: people who work, people who are not allowed to, and people who don't have to.

Elvis Costello

❧ ❧ ❧ ❧

TRYING is the first step towards failure.

Matt Groening

❧ ❧ ❧ ❧

LIFE IS A GREAT surprise. I do not see why death should not be an even greater one.

Vladimir Nabokov

❧ ❧ ❧ ❧

UNTIL I REALIZED that rock music was my connection to the rest of the human race, I felt like I was dying, for some reason, and I didn't really know why.

Bruce Springsteen

❧ ❧ ❧ ❧

YOU MAY NEVER get to touch the Master, but you can tickle his creatures.

Thomas Pynchon

❧ ❧ ❧ ❧

EXTRAORDINARY claims require extraordinary evidence.

Carl Sagan

❧ ❧ ❧ ❧

SUCCESS IS THAT old A B C: ability, breaks, and courage.

Charles Luckman

❧ ❧ ❧ ❧

IF YOU ASK ME what I came to do in this world, I, an artist, will answer you: "I am here to live out loud."

Émile Zola

❧ ❧ ❧ ❧

THERE IS IN THIS world no such force as the force of a man determined to rise.

W.E.B. DuBois

❧ ❧ ❧ ❧

THE GREATEST WAY to live with honor in this world is to be what we pretend to be.

Socrates

❧ ❧ ❧ ❧

IF YOU WON'T be better tomorrow than you were today, then what do you need tomorrow for?

Rabbi Nachman of Bratslav

❧ ❧ ❧ ❧

LIFE DOES NOT consist mainly—or even largely—of facts and happenings. It consists mainly of the storm of thoughts that is forever blowing through one's head.

Mark Twain

❧ ❧ ❧ ❧

THE LONGEST ABSENCE is less perilous to love than the terrible trials of incessant proximity.

Ouida

❧ ❧ ❧ ❧

"REAL ISN'T HOW YOU ARE MADE," said the Skin Horse. "It's a thing that happens to you. When a child loves you for a long, long time, not just to play with but really loves you, then you become Real."

Margery Williams

❧ ❧ ❧ ❧

WE HAVE FORGOTTEN how to be good guests, how to walk lightly on the earth as its other creatures do.

Barbara Ward

❧ ❧ ❧ ❧

DO I DARE
Disturb the universe?

T. S. Eliot

❧ ❧ ❧ ❧

GUTENBERG MADE everybody a reader. Xerox makes everybody a publisher.

Marshall McLuhan

❧ ❧ ❧ ❧

I'M NOT AFRAID of storms, for I'm learning how to sail my ship.

Louisa May Alcott

❧ ❧ ❧ ❧

MISTAKES ARE A PART of being human. Appreciate your mistakes for what they are: Precious life lessons that can only be learned the hard way. Unless it's a fatal mistake, which, at least, others can learn from.

Al Franken

✤ ✤ ✤ ✤

THREE THINGS cannot long be hidden: The sun, the moon, and the truth.

Confucius

✤ ✤ ✤ ✤

IF YOU ASK PEOPLE what they've always wanted to do, most people haven't done it. That breaks my heart.

Angelina Jolie

✤ ✤ ✤ ✤

HISTORY IS THE ESSENCE of innumerable biographies.

Thomas Carlyle

✤ ✤ ✤ ✤

THE GREAT USE OF LIFE is to spend it for something that will outlast it.

William James

✤ ✤ ✤ ✤

GAMES ARE A COMPROMISE between intimacy and keeping intimacy away.

Eric Berne

✤ ✤ ✤ ✤

SOMETIMES, WHEN ONE person is missing, the whole world seems depopulated.

Alphonse de Lamartine

⚜ ⚜ ⚜ ⚜

SPORTS DO NOT build character. They reveal it.

Heywood Brown

⚜ ⚜ ⚜ ⚜

THEY SICKEN of the calm that know the storm.

Dorothy Parker

⚜ ⚜ ⚜ ⚜

IT'S EASIER TO HAVE the vigor of youth when you're old than the wisdom of age when you're young.

Richard J. Needham

⚜ ⚜ ⚜ ⚜

NEARLY ALL MARRIAGES, even happy ones, are mistakes: in the sense that almost certainly (in a more perfect world, or even with a little more care in this very imperfect one) both partners might be found more suitable mates. But the real soul-mate is the one you are actually married to.

J.R.R. Tolkien

⚜ ⚜ ⚜ ⚜

I DREAM, therefore I exist.

August Strindberg

⚜ ⚜ ⚜ ⚜

WE LIVE AND LEARN, but not the wiser grow.

John Pomfret

⚜ ⚜ ⚜ ⚜

NO BIRD SOARS too high if he soars with his own wings.

J. M. Power

⚜ ⚜ ⚜ ⚜

THE ONLY PEOPLE for me are the mad ones, the ones who are mad to live, mad to talk, mad to be saved, desirous of everything at the same time, the ones who never yawn or say a commonplace thing, but burn, burn, burn like fabulous yellow roman candles exploding like spiders across the stars and in the middle you see the blue centerlight pop and everybody goes "Awww!"

Jack Kerouac

⚜ ⚜ ⚜ ⚜

WHAT—me worry?

Harvey Kurtzman

⚜ ⚜ ⚜ ⚜

YOU CAN ONLY find truth with logic if you have already found truth without it.

G. K. Chesterton

⚜ ⚜ ⚜ ⚜

I AM a part of all that I have met.

Alfred Lord Tennyson

⚜ ⚜ ⚜ ⚜

MEN ARE CRUEL, but Man is kind.

Rabindranath Tagore

❖ ❖ ❖ ❖

A GENIUS IS A MAN who has two great ideas.

Jacob Bronowski

❖ ❖ ❖ ❖

TO DREAM OF the person you would like to be is to waste the person you are.

Anonymous

❖ ❖ ❖ ❖

THE BEST ADVICE I can give is to ignore advice. Life is too short to be distracted by the opinions of others.

Russell Edson

❖ ❖ ❖ ❖

HOW OLD WOULD you be if you didn't know how old you are?

Satchel Paige

❖ ❖ ❖ ❖

IF PEOPLE NEVER vanished like the dew of Adashino, never disappeared like the smoke over Toribeyama, how little power to move us could anything possess. The most precious thing about life is its uncertainty.

Yoshida Kenko

❖ ❖ ❖ ❖

THERE'S NO ABSOLUTE freedom anywhere in the world. Freedom is always relative.

Zhang Jie

❧ ❧ ❧ ❧

WHEN YOU HAVE got an elephant by the hind leg, and he is trying to run away, it is best to let him run.

Abraham Lincoln

❧ ❧ ❧ ❧

THE SPIRIT OF LIBERTY is the spirit which is not too sure that it is right.

Learned Hand

❧ ❧ ❧ ❧

I LEARNED . . . that one can never go back, that one should not ever try to go back—the essence of life is going forward. Life is really a One Way Street.

Agatha Christie

❧ ❧ ❧ ❧

I CAN GENERALLY bear the separation, but I don't like the leave-taking.

Samuel Butler

❧ ❧ ❧ ❧

ONE IS ALWAYS a long way from solving a problem until one actually has the answer.

Stephen Hawking

❧ ❧ ❧ ❧

ONE TIME A GUY handed me a picture of himself, and said, "Here's a picture of me when I was younger." Every picture of you is of when you were younger.

Mitch Hedberg

⚜ ⚜ ⚜ ⚜

THE OBJECT of art is to give life shape.

Jean Anouilh

⚜ ⚜ ⚜ ⚜

YOU CANNOT BE MAD at somebody who makes you laugh—it's as simple as that.

Jay Leno

⚜ ⚜ ⚜ ⚜

HOW IS IT THAT our memory is good enough to retain the least triviality that happens to us, and yet not good enough to recollect how often we have told it to the same person?

François de La Rochefoucauld

⚜ ⚜ ⚜ ⚜

EVERYBODY HAS THE BLUES—that's what it comes down to.

James Taylor

⚜ ⚜ ⚜ ⚜

LOSING AN ILLUSION makes you wiser than finding a truth.

Ludwig Börne

⚜ ⚜ ⚜ ⚜

SHE KNOWS WHO she is because she knows who she isn't.

Nikki Giovanni

❧ ❧ ❧ ❧

OPTIMISM IS THE madness of maintaining that everything is right when it is wrong.

Voltaire

❧ ❧ ❧ ❧

ONCE MEN TURNED their thinking over to machines in the hope that this would set them free. But that only permitted other men with machines to enslave them.

Frank Herbert

❧ ❧ ❧ ❧

SPEECHES ARE LIKE steer horns—a point here, a point there, and a lot of bull in between.

Evelyn Anderson

❧ ❧ ❧ ❧

IF A MAN HASN'T discovered something he will die for, he isn't fit to live.

Dr. Martin Luther King, Jr.

❧ ❧ ❧ ❧

TO INSULT SOMEONE we call him "bestial." For deliberate cruelty and nature, "human" might be the greater insult.

Isaac Asimov

❧ ❧ ❧ ❧

DREAM AS IF you'll live forever. Live as if you'll die today.

James Dean

❧ ❧ ❧ ❧

I DON'T KNOW as I want a lawyer to tell me what I cannot do. I hire him to tell me how to do what I want to do.

J. P. Morgan

❧ ❧ ❧ ❧

BY WORKING FAITHFULLY eight hours a day, you may eventually get to be a boss and work twelve hours a day.

Robert Frost

❧ ❧ ❧ ❧

LIFE—THE WAY IT REALLY IS—is a battle not between Bad and Good but between Bad and Worse.

Joseph Brodsky

❧ ❧ ❧ ❧

AMUSEMENT IS THE happiness of those who cannot think.

Alexander Pope

❧ ❧ ❧ ❧

IF IT'S TRUE THAT our species is alone in the universe, then I'd have to say that the universe aimed rather low and settled for very little.

George Carlin

❧ ❧ ❧ ❧

JUSTICE LIMPS ALONG, but it gets there all the same.

Gabriel García Márquez

⚜ ⚜ ⚜ ⚜

HISTORY IS MERELY a list of surprises. It can only prepare us to be surprised yet again.

Kurt Vonnegut

⚜ ⚜ ⚜ ⚜

IN MOST HUMAN AFFAIRS, the idea is to think globally and act locally.

René Dubos

⚜ ⚜ ⚜ ⚜

THE FIFTH AMENDMENT is an old friend and a good friend. It is one of the great landmarks in man's struggle to be free of tyranny, to be decent and civilized. It is our way of escape from the use of torture.

William O. Douglas

⚜ ⚜ ⚜ ⚜

TIME GOES BY: reputation increases, ability declines.

Dag Hammarskjöld

⚜ ⚜ ⚜ ⚜

LOVE MEANS TO LEARN to look at yourself the way one looks at distant things. For you are only one thing among many.

Czeslaw Milosz

⚜ ⚜ ⚜ ⚜

IN MEMORY, everything seems to happen to music.

Tennessee Williams

❖ ❖ ❖ ❖

I HAVE BEEN MISSING the point. The point is not *knowing* another person, or learning to *love* another person. The point is simply this: How tender can we bear to be? What good manners can we show as we welcome ourselves and others into our hearts?

Rebecca Wells

❖ ❖ ❖ ❖

ALL GLORY comes from daring to begin.

Anonymous

❖ ❖ ❖ ❖

A MAN'S MOST valuable trait is a judicious sense of what not to believe.

Euripides

❖ ❖ ❖ ❖

YOU CAN JAIL a revolutionary, but you can't jail a revolution.

Fred Hampton

❖ ❖ ❖ ❖

ARCHITECTURE is the art of how to waste space.

Philip Johnson

❖ ❖ ❖ ❖

ALL PUBLICITY is good, except an obituary notice.

Brendan Behan

✥ ✥ ✥ ✥

PEOPLE WHO DON'T want to get dragged into some kind of work often develop a protective incompetence at it.

Paul Graham

✥ ✥ ✥ ✥

IN AN AGE of universal deceit, telling the truth is a revolutionary act.

George Orwell

✥ ✥ ✥ ✥

LIFE IS A TRAGEDY when seen in close-up, but a comedy in long-shot.

Charlie Chaplin

✥ ✥ ✥ ✥

WHEN A MAN sits with a pretty girl for an hour, it seems like a minute. But let him sit on a hot stove for a minute—and it's longer than any hour. That's relativity.

Albert Einstein

✥ ✥ ✥ ✥

THE AVERAGE MAN, who does not know what to do with his life, wants another one which will last forever.

Anatole France

✥ ✥ ✥ ✥

ANY IDIOT CAN FACE a crisis—it's this day-to-day living that wears you out.

Anton Chekhov

⚜ ⚜ ⚜ ⚜

CONSISTENCY REQUIRES you to be as ignorant today as you were a year ago.

Bernard Berenson

⚜ ⚜ ⚜ ⚜

BEWARE LEST YOU LOSE the substance by grasping at the shadow.

Aesop

⚜ ⚜ ⚜ ⚜

POLITICS is not an exact science.

Otto von Bismarck

⚜ ⚜ ⚜ ⚜

YOU CAN PRETEND to be serious; you can't pretend to be witty.

Sacha Guitry

⚜ ⚜ ⚜ ⚜

I SEE LITTLE OF MORE importance to the future of our country and our civilization than full recognition of the place of the artist. If art is to nourish the roots of our culture, society must set the artist free to follow his vision wherever it takes him.

John F. Kennedy

⚜ ⚜ ⚜ ⚜

THERE IS NOTHING so useless as doing efficiently that which should not be done at all.

Peter Drucker

❧ ❧ ❧ ❧

IT'S MY BELIEF we developed language because of our deep inner need to complain.

Lily Tomlin

❧ ❧ ❧ ❧

THE ARTIST, like the God of the creation, remains within or behind or beyond or above his handiwork, invisible, refined out of existence, indifferent, paring his fingernails.

James Joyce

❧ ❧ ❧ ❧

I FINALLY FIGURED out the only reason to be alive is to enjoy it.

Rita Mae Brown

❧ ❧ ❧ ❧

IF YOU EVER NEED a helping hand, you'll find one at the end of your arm.

Yiddish proverb

❧ ❧ ❧ ❧

WHEN WE HAVE provided against cold, hunger, and thirst, all the rest is but vanity and excess.

Seneca

❧ ❧ ❧ ❧

SOME BOYS ARE born stupid; some achieve stupidity; and some have stupidity thrust upon them.

Samuel Butler

⚜ ⚜ ⚜ ⚜

REALITY IS NOTHING but a collective hunch.

Lily Tomlin

⚜ ⚜ ⚜ ⚜

CLEANING THE HOUSE while your kids are still growing is like shoveling the walk before it stops snowing.

Phyllis Diller

⚜ ⚜ ⚜ ⚜

WHAT IS a rebel? A man who says no.

Albert Camus

⚜ ⚜ ⚜ ⚜

DO WHAT YOU can, with what you have, where you are.

Theodore Roosevelt

⚜ ⚜ ⚜ ⚜

I WOULD INDEED that love were longer-lived,
And vows were not so brittle as they are,
But so it is, and nature has contrived
To struggle on without a break thus far,—
Whether or not we find what we are seeking
Is idle, biologically speaking.

Edna St. Vincent Millay

⚜ ⚜ ⚜ ⚜

WRITERS ARE always selling someone out.

Joan Didion

❧ ❧ ❧ ❧

DELIBERATION IS THE work of many men. Action, of one alone.

Charles de Gaulle

❧ ❧ ❧ ❧

WE PROMISE ACCORDING to our hopes, and perform according to our fears.

François de La Rochefoucauld

❧ ❧ ❧ ❧

THE ROAD WAS new to me, as roads always are going back.

Sarah Orne Jewett

❧ ❧ ❧ ❧

EVERY NOW AND THEN, when you're on stage, you hear the best sound a player can hear. It's a sound you can't get in movies or in television. It is the sound of a wonderful, deep silence that means you've hit them where they live.

Shelley Winters

❧ ❧ ❧ ❧

SO MUCH OF WHAT we call management consists in making it difficult for people to work.

Peter Drucker

❧ ❧ ❧ ❧

HARMONY IS PURE love, for love is complete agreement.

Lope de Vega

❧ ❧ ❧ ❧

HUMAN HISTORY becomes more and more a race between education and catastrophe.

H. G. Wells

❧ ❧ ❧ ❧

NOTHING SO NEEDS reforming as other people's habits.

Mark Twain

❧ ❧ ❧ ❧

IMAGINATION is the highest kite that can fly.

Lauren Bacall

❧ ❧ ❧ ❧

THERE'S NOTHING to writing. All you do is sit down at a type-writer and open a vein.

Walter "Red" Smith

❧ ❧ ❧ ❧

I EXPECT TO PASS through this world but once. Any good therefore that I can do, or any kindness that I can show to any fellow creature, let me do it now. Let me not defer or neglect it, for I shall not pass this way again.

Stephen Grellet

❧ ❧ ❧ ❧

IGNORANCE is a voluntary misfortune.

Nicholas Ling

⚜ ⚜ ⚜ ⚜

WE LEARN BY PRACTICE. Whether it means to learn to dance by practicing dancing or to live by practicing living, the principles are the same.... One becomes, in some area, an athlete of God.

Martha Graham

⚜ ⚜ ⚜ ⚜

ALWAYS GIVE YOUR BEST, never get discouraged, never be petty; always remember, others may hate you, but those who hate you don't win unless you hate them, and then you destroy yourself.

Richard Nixon

⚜ ⚜ ⚜ ⚜

IF EVERYTHING seems under control, you're just not going fast enough.

Mario Andretti

⚜ ⚜ ⚜ ⚜

CONSCIENCE is a mother-in-law whose visit never ends.

H. L. Mencken

⚜ ⚜ ⚜ ⚜

A MAN'S ERRORS are his portals of discovery.

James Joyce

⚜ ⚜ ⚜ ⚜

LET US MAKE a special effort to learn to stop communicating with each other, so we can have some conversation.

Miss Manners (Judith Martin)

⚜ ⚜ ⚜ ⚜

WHEN A THING is done, it's done. Don't look back. Look forward to your next objective.

George C. Marshall

⚜ ⚜ ⚜ ⚜

ALL CITIES ARE MAD, but the madness is gallant. All cities are beautiful, but the beauty is grim.

Christopher Morley

⚜ ⚜ ⚜ ⚜

IF A MAN does not know to what port he is steering, no wind is favorable to him.

Seneca

⚜ ⚜ ⚜ ⚜

IN THIS COUNTRY we encourage "creativity" among the mediocre, but real bursting creativity appalls us. We put it down as undisciplined, as somehow "too much."

Pauline Kael

⚜ ⚜ ⚜ ⚜

IMAGINATION rules the world.

Napoléon Bonaparte

⚜ ⚜ ⚜ ⚜

DEATH IS NOT an event in life: We do not live to experience death.

Ludwig Wittgenstein

⚜ ⚜ ⚜ ⚜

LIFE IS AN adventure in forgiveness.

Norman Cousins

⚜ ⚜ ⚜ ⚜

ART IS significant deformity.

Roger Fry

⚜ ⚜ ⚜ ⚜

EVERY STORY has three sides to it—yours, mine, and the facts.

Foster Meharny Russell

⚜ ⚜ ⚜ ⚜

ONE MUST ABANDON every attempt to make something of oneself, even to make of oneself a righteous person.

Dietrich Bonhoeffer

⚜ ⚜ ⚜ ⚜

THE ROAD GOES ever on and on
Down from the door where it began.
Now far ahead the Road has gone,
And I must follow, if I can,
Pursuing it with eager feet,
Until it joins some larger way
Where many paths and errands meet.
And whither then? I cannot say.

J.R.R. Tolkien

⚜ ⚜ ⚜ ⚜

WE ARE now in the Me Decade.

Tom Wolfe

❧ ❧ ❧ ❧

WAR IS NOT healthy for children and other living things.

Lorraine Schneider

❧ ❧ ❧ ❧

I KNOW GOD will not give me anything I can't handle. I just wish that He didn't trust me so much.

Mother Teresa

❧ ❧ ❧ ❧

EVERYTHING that rises must converge.

Pierre Teilhard de Chardin

❧ ❧ ❧ ❧

NO MAN CAN lose what he never had.

Izaak Walton

❧ ❧ ❧ ❧

TO THOSE WHO do not know mathematics it is difficult to get across a real feeling as to the beauty, the deepest beauty of nature .... If you want to learn about nature, to appreciate nature, it is necessary to understand the language that she speaks in.

Richard P. Feynman

❧ ❧ ❧ ❧

A FRIEND is a gift you give yourself.

Robert Louis Stevenson

❧ ❧ ❧ ❧

LOVE CONQUERS all things except poverty and toothache.

Mae West

❧ ❧ ❧ ❧

ALL CHILDREN, except one, grow up.

James M. Barrie

❧ ❧ ❧ ❧

MY ONLY SKETCH, profile, of Heaven is a large blue sky, bluer and larger than the biggest I have seen in June—and in it are my friends—all of them—every one of them.

Emily Dickinson

❧ ❧ ❧ ❧

ELOQUENCE IS A PAINTING of thought; and thus those who, after having painted it, add something more, make a picture instead of a portrait.

Blaise Pascal

❧ ❧ ❧ ❧

IT TAKES A GREAT deal of bravery to stand up to our enemies, but just as much to stand up to our friends.

J. K. Rowling

❧ ❧ ❧ ❧

LIFE HAS NO MEANING beyond this reality. But people keep searching for excuses. First there was reincarnation. Then refabrication. Now there are theories of life after amoebas, after death, between death, around death.... People call it truth, religion; I call it insanity, the denial of death as the basic truth of life. "What is the meaning of life?" is a stupid question. Life just exists.

Jackie Mason

❧ ❧ ❧ ❧

MAN IS WHAT he believes.

Anton Chekhov

❧ ❧ ❧ ❧

A PARANOID IS A MAN who knows a little of what's going on.

William S. Burroughs

❧ ❧ ❧ ❧

PERSPECTIVE is worth 80 I.Q. points.

Alan Kay

❧ ❧ ❧ ❧

GOD GAVE US MEMORY so that we might have roses in December.

James M. Barrie

❧ ❧ ❧ ❧

HISTORY is more or less bunk.

Henry Ford

❧ ❧ ❧ ❧

THEY KNOW enough who know how to learn.

Henry Adams

❧ ❧ ❧ ❧

CONCISENESS is the sister of talent.

Anton Chekhov

❧ ❧ ❧ ❧

TO CONSIDER ONESELF different from ordinary men is wrong, but it is right to hope that one will not remain like ordinary men.

Yoshida Shoin

❧ ❧ ❧ ❧

THE FUTURE is already here. It's just not very evenly distributed.

William Gibson

❧ ❧ ❧ ❧

A MAN MAY FULFILL the object of his existence by asking a question he cannot answer, and attempting a task he cannot achieve.

Oliver Wendell Holmes

❧ ❧ ❧ ❧

THE KEY TO REALIZING a dream is to focus not on success but on significance—and then even the small steps and little victories along your path will take on greater meaning.

Oprah Winfrey

❧ ❧ ❧ ❧

THE INTERNET is an elite organization; most of the population of the world has never even made a phone call.

Noam Chomsky

❖ ❖ ❖ ❖

SERVICE is the rent we pay for living.

Marian Wright Edelman

❖ ❖ ❖ ❖

ALL VISIBLE OBJECTS, man, are but as pasteboard masks.... Strike, strike through the mask!

Herman Melville

❖ ❖ ❖ ❖

NO RAIN, no rainbows.

Anonymous

❖ ❖ ❖ ❖

EVERYTHING SHOULD be made as simple as possible, but not simpler.

Albert Einstein

❖ ❖ ❖ ❖

GROWN-UPS NEVER understand anything for themselves, and it is tiresome for children to be always and forever explaining things to them.

Antoine de Saint-Exupéry

❖ ❖ ❖ ❖

PUNCTUALITY IS the virtue of the bored.

Evelyn Waugh

❧ ❧ ❧ ❧

MEDICINE IS MY lawful wife. Literature is my mistress.

Anton Chekhov

❧ ❧ ❧ ❧

WE DO NOT SEE things as they are, but as we are ourselves.

Henry M. Tomlinson

❧ ❧ ❧ ❧

LET US ACT ON what we have, since we have not what we wish.

Cardinal John Henry Newman

❧ ❧ ❧ ❧

IF YOU WERE A BIRD, and lived on high,
You'd lean on the wind when the wind came by,
You'd say to the wind when it took you away:
"*That's* where I wanted to go today!"

A. A. Milne

❧ ❧ ❧ ❧

WHAT'S WRONG with dropping out? To me, this is the whole
point: one's right to withdraw from a social environment that
offers no spiritual sustenance, and to mind one's own business.

William S. Burroughs

❧ ❧ ❧ ❧

I DO NOT KNOW much about gods; but I think that the river is a strong brown god—sullen, untamed, and intractable.

T. S. Eliot

❧ ❧ ❧ ❧

WHAT I CANNOT create I do not understand.

Richard P. Feynman

❧ ❧ ❧ ❧

GO TO WHERE the silence is and say something.

Amy Goodman

❧ ❧ ❧ ❧

IF YOU STEAL from one author, it's plagiarism; if you steal from many, it's research.

Wilson Mizner

❧ ❧ ❧ ❧

WHENEVER SCIENCE makes a discovery, the devil grabs it while the angels are debating the best way to use it.

Alan Valentine

❧ ❧ ❧ ❧

ADULTHOOD IS THE ever-shrinking period between childhood and old age. It is the apparent aim of modern industrial societies to reduce this period to a minimum.

Thomas Szasz

❧ ❧ ❧ ❧

LONG AFTER THE BOMB falls and you and your good deeds are gone, cockroaches will still be here, prowling the street like armored cars.

Tama Janowitz

❧ ❧ ❧ ❧

LIBERTY DOESN'T WORK as well in practice as it does in speeches.

Will Rogers

❧ ❧ ❧ ❧

NOBODY EVER LIVES their life all the way up except bullfighters.

Ernest Hemingway

❧ ❧ ❧ ❧

WHEN ALL THE TREES have been cut down, when all the animals have been hunted, when all the waters are polluted, when all the air is unsafe to breathe, only then will you discover you cannot eat money.

Cree prophecy

❧ ❧ ❧ ❧

WHEN YOU ARE good to others, you are best to yourself.

Benjamin Franklin

❧ ❧ ❧ ❧

IMAGINATION is the true magic carpet.

Norman Vincent Peale

❧ ❧ ❧ ❧

A MINIMUM OF COMFORT is necessary for the practice of virtue.

Patrice Lumumba

❧ ❧ ❧ ❧

AS A WELL-SPENT day brings happy sleep, so life well used brings happy death.

Leonardo da Vinci

❧ ❧ ❧ ❧

DO AS YOU WOULD be done by is the surest method that I know of pleasing.

Philip Dormer Stanhope (Lord Chesterfield)

❧ ❧ ❧ ❧

AS THE TRAVELER who has been once from home is wiser than he who has never left his own door step, so a knowledge of one other culture should sharpen our ability to scrutinize more steadily, to appreciate more lovingly, our own.

Margaret Mead

❧ ❧ ❧ ❧

NEVER RUIN an apology with an excuse.

Kimberly Johnson

❧ ❧ ❧ ❧

THE MORE LAWS and order are made prominent, the more thieves and robbers there will be.

Lao Tzu

❧ ❧ ❧ ❧

THE FOUR MOST beautiful words in our common language:
I told you so.

Gore Vidal

❧ ❧ ❧ ❧

THE AVERAGE MAN doesn't want to be free. He simply wants to
be safe.

H. L. Mencken

❧ ❧ ❧ ❧

ONE KEEPS ON FORGETTING old age up to the very brink of the
grave.

Colette

❧ ❧ ❧ ❧

THE HUMAN RACE has one really effective weapon, and that is
laughter.

Mark Twain

❧ ❧ ❧ ❧

WHEN YOU BUY, use your eyes and your mind, not your ears.

Anonymous

❧ ❧ ❧ ❧

WHEN, A SMALL CHILD, I was rambling over there by the fir
trees, I thought that success spelled happiness. I was wrong.
Happiness is like a butterfly that appears and delights us for
one brief moment, but soon flits away.

Anna Pavlova

❧ ❧ ❧ ❧

WHERE NO ONE intrudes, many can live in harmony.

Chief Dan George

❖ ❖ ❖ ❖

BEING DEFEATED is only a temporary condition; giving up is what makes it permanent.

Marilyn vos Savant

❖ ❖ ❖ ❖

EXPECTATIONS IS THE PLACE you must always go to before you get to where you're going. Of course, some people never go beyond Expectations, but my job is to hurry them along whether they like it or not.

Norton Juster

❖ ❖ ❖ ❖

SMART WOMEN LOVE smart men more than smart men love smart women.

Natalie Portman

❖ ❖ ❖ ❖

THE ONLY REASON some people get lost in thought is because it's unfamiliar territory.

Paul Fix

❖ ❖ ❖ ❖

NATURE CONCEALS her secrets because she is sublime, not because she is a trickster.

Albert Einstein

❖ ❖ ❖ ❖

FREEDOM IS NOTHING else but a chance to be better, whereas enslavement is a certainty of the worst.

Albert Camus

⚜ ⚜ ⚜ ⚜

WHEN THE RICH wage war, it's the poor who die.

Jean-Paul Sartre

⚜ ⚜ ⚜ ⚜

MORE THAN KISSES, letters mingle souls.

John Donne

⚜ ⚜ ⚜ ⚜

HALF THE HARM that is done in this world is due to people who want to feel important. They don't mean to do harm—but the harm does not interest them. Or they do not see it, or they justify it, because they are absorbed in the endless struggle to think well of themselves.

T. S. Eliot

⚜ ⚜ ⚜ ⚜

A PERSON'S MIND stretched to a new idea never goes back to its original dimensions.

Oliver Wendell Holmes, Jr.

⚜ ⚜ ⚜ ⚜

THE BEST AD is a good product.

Alan H. Meyer

⚜ ⚜ ⚜ ⚜

I HAVE NEVER in my life learned anything from any man who agreed with me.

Dudley Field Malone

✣ ✣ ✣ ✣

WE WILL either find a way, or make one.

Hannibal

✣ ✣ ✣ ✣

NO MATTER WHERE you go or what you do, you live your entire life within the confines of your head.

Terry Josephson

✣ ✣ ✣ ✣

WE WASTE A LOT of time running after people we could have caught by just standing still.

Mignon McLaughlin

✣ ✣ ✣ ✣

IT IS NEVER a waste of time to study the history of a word.

Lucien Febvre

✣ ✣ ✣ ✣

LIFE IS A HOSPITAL in which every patient is possessed by the desire to change his bed. This one would prefer to suffer near the fire, and that one is certain he would get well if he were by the window.

Charles Baudelaire

✣ ✣ ✣ ✣

INSTANT gratification takes too long.

Carrie Fisher

❧ ❧ ❧ ❧

THE TROUBLE with our times is that the future is not what it used to be.

Paul Valéry

❧ ❧ ❧ ❧

FOR WHAT YOU have tamed, you become responsible forever.

Antoine de Saint-Exupéry

❧ ❧ ❧ ❧

HE LOOKED DOWN the slope and, at the base, in the shadow of the wall of the Park, he saw some human figures lying. Those venal and furtive loves filled him with despair. He gnawed the rectitude of his life; he felt that he had been outcast from life's feast.

James Joyce

❧ ❧ ❧ ❧

A HUMORIST IS A MAN who feels bad but who feels good about it.

Don Herold

❧ ❧ ❧ ❧

ALMOST ALL CRIME is due to the repressed desire for aesthetic expression.

Evelyn Waugh

❧ ❧ ❧ ❧

HUMAN BEINGS have an inalienable right to invent themselves.

Germaine Greer

❖ ❖ ❖ ❖

THE INSTINCT OF NEARLY all societies is to lock up anybody who is truly free. First, society begins by trying to beat you up. If this fails, they try to poison you. If this fails too, they finish by loading honors on your head.

Jean Cocteau

❖ ❖ ❖ ❖

TO FLY, we have to have resistance.

Maya Lin

❖ ❖ ❖ ❖

LEAD ME NOT into temptation; I can find the way there myself.

Rita Mae Brown

❖ ❖ ❖ ❖

IN THE BOOK of life, the answers aren't in the back.

Charles Schulz

❖ ❖ ❖ ❖

WE MUST AS a second best, as people say, take the least of the evils.

Aristotle

❖ ❖ ❖ ❖

AN APPEASER is one who feeds a crocodile—hoping that it will eat him last.

Winston Churchill

❧ ❧ ❧ ❧

OUR LIVES BEGIN to end the day we become silent about things that matter.

Dr. Martin Luther King, Jr.

❧ ❧ ❧ ❧

TEMPTATIONS CAN be got rid of. How? By yielding to them.

Honoré de Balzac

❧ ❧ ❧ ❧

LEISURE is the mother of Philosophy.

Thomes Hobbes

❧ ❧ ❧ ❧

WE CAMPAIGN IN POETRY, but when we're elected we're forced to govern in prose.

Mario Cuomo

❧ ❧ ❧ ❧

WHEN YOU PLAY from your heart, all of a sudden there's no gravity. You don't feel the weight of the world, of bills, of anything. That's why people love it. Your so-called insurmountable problems disappear, and instead of problems you get possibilities.

Carlos Santana

❧ ❧ ❧ ❧

SERIOUS SPORT has nothing to do with fair play. It is bound up with hatred, jealousy, boastfulness, disregard of all rules, and sadistic pleasure in witnessing violence: In other words, it is war minus the shooting.

George Orwell

⚜ ⚜ ⚜ ⚜

EITHER YOU DECIDE to stay in the shallow end of the pool or you go out in the ocean.

Christopher Reeve

⚜ ⚜ ⚜ ⚜

TO DO GREAT THINGS is difficult, but to command great things is more difficult.

Friedrich Nietzsche

⚜ ⚜ ⚜ ⚜

FEAR IS THE OLDEST and strongest emotion of mankind.

H. P. Lovecraft

⚜ ⚜ ⚜ ⚜

A MAN SHOULD have the fine point of his soul taken off to become fit for this world.

John Keats

⚜ ⚜ ⚜ ⚜

THE HALLS OF JUSTICE. That's the only place you see the justice, is in the halls.

Lenny Bruce

⚜ ⚜ ⚜ ⚜

DO NOT SEEK to follow in the footsteps of the men of old; seek what they sought.

Matsuo Basho

❧ ❧ ❧ ❧

THUNDER IS GOOD, thunder is impressive; but it is lightning that does the work.

Mark Twain

❧ ❧ ❧ ❧

NOTHING is so much to be feared as fear.

Henry David Thoreau

❧ ❧ ❧ ❧

DEVELOP INTEREST in life as you see it; in people, things, literature, music—the world is so rich, simply throbbing with rich treasures, beautiful souls, and interesting people. Forget yourself.

Henry Miller

❧ ❧ ❧ ❧

THERE ARE TWO kinds of lawyers: one who knows the law, the other who knows the judge.

Joseph H. Choate

❧ ❧ ❧ ❧

A MAN ALWAYS has two reasons for what he does—a good one, and the real one.

J. P. Morgan

❧ ❧ ❧ ❧

LIFE IS UNCERTAIN. Eat dessert first.

Ernestine Ulmer

⚜ ⚜ ⚜ ⚜

GENUINE TRAGEDIES in the world are not conflicts between right and wrong. They are conflicts between two rights.

Georg Wilhelm Friedrich Hegel

⚜ ⚜ ⚜ ⚜

THE SALARY OF THE chief executive of the large corporation is not a market award for achievement. It is frequently in the nature of a warm personal gesture by the individual to himself.

John Kenneth Galbraith

⚜ ⚜ ⚜ ⚜

ABOUT THE ONLY thing that comes to us without effort is old age.

Gloria Pitzer

⚜ ⚜ ⚜ ⚜

CONSCIENCE AND COWARDICE are really the same things.... Conscience is the trade-name of the firm.

Oscar Wilde

⚜ ⚜ ⚜ ⚜

EVERYTHING IS FUNNY as long as it is happening to somebody else.

Will Rogers

⚜ ⚜ ⚜ ⚜

YOU'RE TRYING to live without enemies. That's all you think about, not having enemies.

Isaac Babel

❧ ❧ ❧ ❧

MAN IS FREE the moment he wishes to be.

Voltaire

❧ ❧ ❧ ❧

LIFE IS A ZOO in a jungle.

Peter de Vries

❧ ❧ ❧ ❧

A LIBRARY doesn't need windows. A library is a window.

Stewart Brand

❧ ❧ ❧ ❧

GO FORWARD with courage. When you are in doubt be still and wait; when doubt no longer exists for you, then go forward with courage. So long as mists envelop you, be still; be still until the sunlight pours through and dispels the mists—as it surely will. Then act with courage.

White Eagle

❧ ❧ ❧ ❧

HAPPINESS IS BENEFICIAL to the body, but it is grief that develops the powers of the mind.

Marcel Proust

❧ ❧ ❧ ❧

I TAKE A SIMPLE view of living. It is keep your eyes open and get on with it.

Laurence Olivier

❖ ❖ ❖ ❖

I AM FREE of all prejudice. I hate everyone equally.

W. C. Fields

❖ ❖ ❖ ❖

BEING POWERFUL is like being a lady. If you have to tell people you are, you aren't.

Margaret Thatcher

❖ ❖ ❖ ❖

WE ALL LIVE in a house on fire, no fire department to call; no way out, just the upstairs window to look out of while the fire burns the house down with us trapped, locked in it.

Tennessee Williams

❖ ❖ ❖ ❖

NEVER BELIEVE in mirrors or newspapers.

Tom Stoppard

❖ ❖ ❖ ❖

AN EXPERT is a man who has made all the mistakes which can be made, in a very narrow field.

Niels Bohr

❖ ❖ ❖ ❖

JUDGE NO MAN before you have walked for two moons in his moccasins.

Native American proverb

❖ ❖ ❖ ❖

NO ENTERTAINMENT is so cheap as reading nor any pleasure so lasting.

Lady Mary Wortley Montagu

❖ ❖ ❖ ❖

I HAVE MISSED more than 9,000 shots in my career. I have lost almost 300 games. On 26 occasions I have been entrusted to take the game winning shot...and I missed. I have failed over and over and over again in my life. And that's precisely why I succeed.

Michael Jordan

❖ ❖ ❖ ❖

MAN APPEARS to be the missing link between anthropoid apes and human beings.

Konrad Lorenz

❖ ❖ ❖ ❖

THE HONESTER the man, the worse the luck.

John Ray

❖ ❖ ❖ ❖

THE FIRST CONDITION of progress is the removal of censorship.

George Bernard Shaw

❖ ❖ ❖ ❖

ANGELS CAN FLY because they take themselves lightly.

G. K. Chesterton

⚜ ⚜ ⚜ ⚜

IF YOU DON'T risk anything, you risk even more.

Erica Jong

⚜ ⚜ ⚜ ⚜

THE GREATEST GIFT is not being afraid to question.

Ruby Dee

⚜ ⚜ ⚜ ⚜

IN ALL THINGS that are purely social we can be as separate as the fingers, yet one as the hand in all things essential to mutual progress.

Booker T. Washington

⚜ ⚜ ⚜ ⚜

FOR MOST MEN, life is a search for the proper manila envelope in which to get themselves filed.

Clifton Fadiman

⚜ ⚜ ⚜ ⚜

I WISH THAT I may never think the smiles of the great and powerful a sufficient inducement to turn aside from the straight path of honesty and the convictions of my own mind.

David Ricardo

⚜ ⚜ ⚜ ⚜

IF YOU MAKE people think they're thinking, they'll love you; but if you really make them think, they'll hate you.

Don Marquis

�֍ ✤ ✤ ✤

IF A MAN WILL begin with certainties, he shall end in doubts, but if he will be content to begin with doubts, he shall end in certainties.

Francis Bacon

✤ ✤ ✤ ✤

IT IS BETTER TO light a candle than to curse the darkness.

Chinese proverb

✤ ✤ ✤ ✤

A MODEST MAN is usually admired—if people ever hear of him.

Edgar Watson Howe

✤ ✤ ✤ ✤

THE FUNDAMENTAL cause of trouble in the world today is that the stupid are cocksure while the intelligent are full of doubt.

Bertrand Russell

✤ ✤ ✤ ✤

TO BE NORMAL is the ultimate aim of the unsuccessful.

Carl Jung

✤ ✤ ✤ ✤

ANYTHING WORTH doing is worth overdoing.

Mick Jagger

⚜ ⚜ ⚜ ⚜

NECESSITY never made a good bargain.

Benjamin Franklin

⚜ ⚜ ⚜ ⚜

IF WE KNEW what it was we were doing, it would not be called research, would it?

Albert Einstein

⚜ ⚜ ⚜ ⚜

THE TRUTH IS that our finest moments are most likely to occur when we are feeling deeply uncomfortable, unhappy, or unfulfilled. For it is only in such moments, propelled by our discomfort, that we are likely to step out of our ruts and start searching for different ways or truer answers.

M. Scott Peck

⚜ ⚜ ⚜ ⚜

WISE MEN LEARN more from fools than fools from wise men.

Cato the Elder

⚜ ⚜ ⚜ ⚜

THE FUTURE is made of the same stuff as the present.

Simone Weil

⚜ ⚜ ⚜ ⚜

A THOUSAND MEN can't undress a naked man.

Greek proverb

❧ ❧ ❧ ❧

ONE DAY ALICE came to a fork in the road and saw a Cheshire cat in a tree. "Which road do I take?" she asked. "Where do you want to go?" was his response. "I don't know," Alice answered. "Then" said the cat, "it doesn't matter."

Lewis Carroll

❧ ❧ ❧ ❧

TO BE AN ARTIST means never to avert one's eyes.

Akira Kurosawa

❧ ❧ ❧ ❧

THE BEST vision is insight.

Malcolm S. Forbes

❧ ❧ ❧ ❧

IF OUR PEOPLE fight one tribe at a time, all will be killed. They can cut off our fingers one by one, but if we join together we will make a powerful fist.

Little Turtle

❧ ❧ ❧ ❧

FORM ever follows function.

Louis H. Sullivan

❧ ❧ ❧ ❧

POLITICIANS WHO complain about the press are like sailors complaining about the weather.

Enoch Powell

❧ ❧ ❧ ❧

MOST MEN, when they think they are thinking, are merely rearranging their prejudices.

Knute Rockne

❧ ❧ ❧ ❧

HOW MUCH REVERENCE can you have for a Supreme Being who finds it necessary to include such phenomena as phlegm and tooth decay in His divine system of creation?

Joseph Heller

❧ ❧ ❧ ❧

YOU CAN'T WIN unless you learn how to lose.

Kareem Abdul-Jabbar

❧ ❧ ❧ ❧

TRUTH IS THE ONLY merit that gives dignity and worth to history.

John Dalberg-Acton (Lord Acton)

❧ ❧ ❧ ❧

ON STAGE I MAKE love to twenty-five thousand people; then I go home alone.

Janis Joplin

❧ ❧ ❧ ❧

LIBERTY CONSISTS in doing what one desires.

John Stuart Mill

❧ ❧ ❧ ❧

WE ALL LIVE under the same sky, but we don't all have the same horizon.

Konrad Adenauer

❧ ❧ ❧ ❧

WE WERE PROCLAIMING ourselves political hypocrites before the world, by thus fostering Human Slavery and proclaiming ourselves, at the same time, the sole friends of Human Freedom.

Abraham Lincoln

❧ ❧ ❧ ❧

TO SWEAR OFF making mistakes is very easy. All you have to do is swear off having ideas.

Leo Burnett

❧ ❧ ❧ ❧

A PAGE OF HISTORY is worth a volume of logic.

Oliver Wendell Holmes

❧ ❧ ❧ ❧

MANY A MAN has fallen in love with a girl in a light so dim he would not have chosen a suit by it.

Maurice Chevalier

❧ ❧ ❧ ❧

ADS PUSH the principle of noise all the way to the plateau of persuasion. They are quite in accord with the procedures of brainwashing.

Marshall McLuhan

❖ ❖ ❖ ❖

THE GREATEST TRUTHS are the simplest, and so are the greatest men.

J. C. and A. W. Hare

❖ ❖ ❖ ❖

SUCCESS is somebody else's failure.

Ursula K. Le Guin

❖ ❖ ❖ ❖

DON'T PART WITH your illusions. When they are gone you may still exist but you will have ceased to live.

Mark Twain

❖ ❖ ❖ ❖

ONLY THE SHALLOW know themselves.

Oscar Wilde

❖ ❖ ❖ ❖

CHARACTER CANNOT be developed in ease and quiet. Only through experiences of trial and suffering can the soul be strengthened, vision cleared, ambition inspired, and success achieved.

Helen Keller

❖ ❖ ❖ ❖

FRIENDSHIP NEEDS no words—it is solitude delivered from the anguish of loneliness.

Dag Hammarskjöld

❧ ❧ ❧ ❧

MY MOUTH SHALL be the mouth of misfortunes which have no mouth, my voice the freedoms of those freedoms which break down in the prison-cell of despair.

Aimé Fernand Césaire

❧ ❧ ❧ ❧

THE STREETS are safe in Philadelphia. It's only the people who make them unsafe.

Frank Rizzo

❧ ❧ ❧ ❧

I DO WANT TO GET RICH, but I never want to do what there is to get rich.

Gertrude Stein

❧ ❧ ❧ ❧

TO KNOCK A THING DOWN, especially if it is cocked at an arrogant angle, is a deep delight to the blood.

George Santayana

❧ ❧ ❧ ❧

THE NICE THING about being a celebrity is that when you bore people, they think it's their fault.

Henry Kissinger

❧ ❧ ❧ ❧

MIDDLE AGE IS WHEN you have a choice of two temptations and choose the one that will get you home earlier.

Anonymous

❧ ❧ ❧ ❧

THE LIFE OF THE GREAT majority is only a constant struggle for this same existence, with the certainty of ultimately losing it.

Arthur Schopenhauer

❧ ❧ ❧ ❧

BEAUTY, MORE THAN bitterness, makes the heart break.

Sara Teasdale

❧ ❧ ❧ ❧

THE COUNTRY HAS CHARMS only for those not obliged to stay there.

Edouard Manet

❧ ❧ ❧ ❧

ALL DREAMS spin out from the same web.

Hopi proverb

❧ ❧ ❧ ❧

MY LIFE HAS BEEN one great big joke,
a dance that's walked, a song that's spoke.
I laugh so hard I almost choke
when I think about myself.

Maya Angelou

❧ ❧ ❧ ❧

ONLY THOSE WHO dare to fail greatly can ever achieve greatly.

Robert F. Kennedy

❖ ❖ ❖ ❖

WE GROW NEITHER better nor worse as we get old, but more like ourselves.

May Lamberton Becker

❖ ❖ ❖ ❖

WRITING IS TURNING one's worst moments into money.

J. P. Donleavy

❖ ❖ ❖ ❖

IT TAKES MORAL courage to grieve. It requires religious courage to rejoice.

Søren Kierkegaard

❖ ❖ ❖ ❖

WE ARE DROWNING in information, while starving for wisdom. The world henceforth will be run by synthesizers, people able to put together the right information at the right time, think critically about it, and make important choices wisely.

Edward O. Wilson

❖ ❖ ❖ ❖

ALL WORDS are pegs to hang ideas on.

Henry Ward Beecher

❖ ❖ ❖ ❖

THOSE WHO LACK the courage will always find a philosophy to justify it.

Albert Camus

❧ ❧ ❧ ❧

THE LESS you know, the more you believe.

Bono (Paul Hewson)

❧ ❧ ❧ ❧

IN ADVERTISING THERE is a saying that if you can keep your head while all those around you are losing theirs—then you just don't understand the problem.

Hugh M. Beville, Jr.

❧ ❧ ❧ ❧

IF A DOG WILL NOT COME to you after having looked you in the face, you should go home and examine your conscience.

Woodrow Wilson

❧ ❧ ❧ ❧

A DESIRE TO TAKE medicine is, perhaps, the great feature which distinguishes man from other animals.

William Osler

❧ ❧ ❧ ❧

WE ARE THE CHILDREN of our landscape.

Lawrence Durrell

❧ ❧ ❧ ❧

IF NOTHING ELSE is left, one must scream. Silence is the real crime against humanity.

Nadezhda Mandelstam

❧ ❧ ❧ ❧

TURN YOUR wounds into wisdom.

Oprah Winfrey

❧ ❧ ❧ ❧

A MAN WHO HAS no imagination has no wings.

Muhammad Ali

❧ ❧ ❧ ❧

ANXIETY IS LOVE's greatest killer. It creates the failures. It makes others feel as you might when a drowning man holds on to you. You want to save him, but you know he will strangle you with his panic.

Anaïs Nin

❧ ❧ ❧ ❧

CIVILITY costs nothing, and buys everything.

Lady Mary Wortley Montagu

❧ ❧ ❧ ❧

IT IS A WHOLESOME and necessary thing for us to turn again to the earth and in the contemplation of her beauties to know the sense of wonder and humility.

Rachel Carson

❧ ❧ ❧ ❧

THE PURPOSE OF LIFE is to reach perfection. The rose starts as a seed or cutting, then grows and prospers with the sunshine and the rain. After a period of time the perfect rose blossoms. The human experience is much the same, except that the time span is much greater because man, before he can reach this state of perfection, must return again and again through many incarnations in order to conquer all disease, greed, jealousy, anger, hatred, and guilt.... He must pattern himself after the masters of perfection, such as the great master Jesus. Wanting to be perfect is all that is required.

Willie Nelson

❧ ❧ ❧ ❧

GREAT AND GOOD are seldom the same man.

Thomas Fuller

❧ ❧ ❧ ❧

HATE THE SIN and love the sinner.

St. Augustine

❧ ❧ ❧ ❧

SOCIAL TACT is making your company feel at home, even though you wish they were.

Anonymous

❧ ❧ ❧ ❧

NO LEGACY is so rich as honesty.

William Shakespeare

❧ ❧ ❧ ❧

I BELIEVE THAT man will not merely endure: He will prevail. He is immortal, not because he alone among creatures has an inexhaustible voice, but because he has a soul, a spirit capable of compassion and sacrifice and endurance.

William Faulkner

❧ ❧ ❧ ❧

SPORTS is human life in microcosm.

Howard Cosell

❧ ❧ ❧ ❧

DEMOCRACY is an abuse of statistics.

Jorge Luis Borges

❧ ❧ ❧ ❧

IF WE ARE TO ACHIEVE results never before accomplished, we must expect to employ methods never before attempted.

Francis Bacon

❧ ❧ ❧ ❧

AGE IS A HIGH price to pay for maturity.

Tom Stoppard

❧ ❧ ❧ ❧

TOO MANY PEOPLE spend money they haven't earned, to buy things they don't want, to impress people they don't like.

Will Smith

❧ ❧ ❧ ❧

EVERYTHING STARTS as somebody's daydream.

Larry Niven

❧ ❧ ❧ ❧

WE CAN DO NO GREAT THINGS—only small things with great love.

Mother Teresa

❧ ❧ ❧ ❧

THE WORST crime is faking it.

Kurt Cobain

❧ ❧ ❧ ❧

DEMOCRACY IS BASED on the assumption that a million men are wiser than one man. How's that again? I missed something?

Robert A. Heinlein

❧ ❧ ❧ ❧

IT IS ERROR ALONE which needs the support of government. Truth can stand by itself.

Thomas Jefferson

❧ ❧ ❧ ❧

ALL TRUE HISTORIES contain instruction; though in some, the treasure may be hard to find, and when found, so trivial in quantity that the dry, shriveled kernel scarcely compensates for the trouble of cracking the nut.

Anne Brontë

❧ ❧ ❧ ❧

MONEY IS NONE of the wheels of trade: It is the oil which renders the motion of the wheels more smooth and easy.

David Hume

❧ ❧ ❧ ❧

WITH SOME PEOPLE solitariness is an escape not from others but from themselves. For they see in the eyes of others only a reflection of themselves.

Eric Hoffer

❧ ❧ ❧ ❧

TAKE NOTHING on its looks; take everything on evidence. There's no better rule.

Charles Dickens

❧ ❧ ❧ ❧

TORTURE NUMBERS, and they'll confess to anything.

Gregg Easterbrook

❧ ❧ ❧ ❧

YOU CAN'T KEEP blaming yourself. Just blame yourself once, and move on.

Homer Simpson (Matt Groening)

❧ ❧ ❧ ❧

THE DIGNITY OF MAN lies in his ability to face reality in all its meaninglessness.

Martin Esslin

❧ ❧ ❧ ❧

WHEN WE TRY to pick out anything by itself we find that it is bound fast by a thousand invisible cords that cannot be broken, to everything in the universe.

John Muir

❖ ❖ ❖ ❖

STYLE is the man himself.

Georges-Louis Leclerc, Comte de Buffon

❖ ❖ ❖ ❖

THE HARDEST JOB kids face today is learning good manners without seeing any.

Fred Astaire

❖ ❖ ❖ ❖

WORK IS LOVE made visible. And if you cannot work with love but only distaste, it is better that you should leave your work and sit at the gate of the temple and take alms of those who work with joy.

Kahlil Gibran

❖ ❖ ❖ ❖

"KNOW THYSELF?" If I knew myself, I'd run away.

Johann Wolfgang von Goethe

❖ ❖ ❖ ❖

HISTORY SHOWS that there are no invincible armies.

Josef Stalin

❖ ❖ ❖ ❖

NO SNOWFLAKE in an avalanche ever feels responsible.

Stanislaw Jerzy Lec

❖ ❖ ❖ ❖

I STOPPED BELIEVING in Santa Claus when I was six. Mother took me to see him in a department store, and he asked for my autograph.

Shirley Temple Black

❖ ❖ ❖ ❖

CONSCIENCE reigns but it does not govern.

Paul Valéry

❖ ❖ ❖ ❖

A MAN WHO LIES, thinking it is the truth, is an honest man, and a man who tells the truth, believing it to be a lie, is a liar.

William Safire

❖ ❖ ❖ ❖

ANY TWO PHILOSOPHERS can tell each other all they know in two hours.

Oliver Wendell Holmes, Jr.

❖ ❖ ❖ ❖

IN MATHEMATICS you don't understand things, you just get used to them.

John von Neumann

❖ ❖ ❖ ❖

I ENVY PEOPLE WHO DRINK. At least they have something to blame everything on.

Oscar Levant

✤ ✤ ✤ ✤

THERE IS NOT A FIERCER HELL than the failure in a great object.

John Keats

✤ ✤ ✤ ✤

YOUR WORLD is as big as you make it.

Georgia Douglas Johnson

✤ ✤ ✤ ✤

NO GRAND IDEA was ever born in a conference, but a lot of foolish ideas have died there.

F. Scott Fitzgerald

✤ ✤ ✤ ✤

WHAT IS LIFE? It is the flash of the firefly in the night. It is the breath of the buffalo in the wintertime. It is the little shadow that runs across the grass and loses itself in the sunset.

Crowfoot

✤ ✤ ✤ ✤

IT'S NOT TRUE that life is one damn thing after another—it's one damn thing over and over.

Edna St. Vincent Millay

✤ ✤ ✤ ✤

THE SINGLE MOST IMPORTANT conclusion I reached, after traveling through Japan—as well as countless hours reading, studying, and analyzing this fascinating culture—is that you should always tighten the cap on the shampoo bottle before you put it in your suitcase.

Dave Barry

✤ ✤ ✤ ✤

I AM WHAT I AM. To look for "reasons" is beside the point.

Joan Didion

✤ ✤ ✤ ✤

REALITY IS THAT WHICH, when you stop believing in it, doesn't go away.

Philip K. Dick

✤ ✤ ✤ ✤

TO US HE [FREUD] IS NO MORE a person now but a whole climate of opinion.

W. H. Auden

✤ ✤ ✤ ✤

DYING is a wild Night and a new Road.

Emily Dickinson

✤ ✤ ✤ ✤

ONE MAN'S quiet is another man's din.

Carrie Latet

✤ ✤ ✤ ✤

EACH NEW GENERATION is a fresh invasion of savages.

Hervey Allen

❧ ❧ ❧ ❧

HALF THE WORLD is composed of people who have something to say and can't, and the other half who have nothing to say and keep on saying it.

Robert Frost

❧ ❧ ❧ ❧

WHISKEY DROWNS some troubles and floats a lot more.

Robert C. Edwards

❧ ❧ ❧ ❧

IT IS BEST TO LOVE WISELY, no doubt; but to love foolishly is better than not to be able to love at all.

William Makepeace Thackeray

❧ ❧ ❧ ❧

TRUTH is such a rare thing, it is delightful to tell it.

Emily Dickinson

❧ ❧ ❧ ❧

I THINK LAUGHTER may be a form of courage.... As humans, we sometimes stand tall and look into the sun and laugh, and I think we are never more brave than when we do that.

Linda Ellerbee

❧ ❧ ❧ ❧

THEY TEACH YOU there's a boundary line to music. But, man, there's no boundary line to art.

Charlie "Bird" Parker

❧ ❧ ❧ ❧

EQUALITY MAY PERHAPS be a right, but no power on earth can ever turn it into a fact.

Honoré de Balzac

❧ ❧ ❧ ❧

THE SECRET OF BUSINESS is to know something that nobody else knows.

Aristotle Onassis

❧ ❧ ❧ ❧

THERE IS NO GREAT GENIUS without a tincture of madness.

Seneca

❧ ❧ ❧ ❧

BROTHER, OUR SEATS were once large, and yours were small. You have now become a great people, and we have scarcely a place left to spread our blankets. You have got our country, but are not satisfied; you want to force your religion upon us.

Red Jacket

❧ ❧ ❧ ❧

ADULTS are obsolete children.

Dr. Seuss

❧ ❧ ❧ ❧

A SINGLE DEATH is a tragedy, a million deaths is a statistic.

Josef Stalin

❧ ❧ ❧ ❧

TRUST YOURSELF. You know more than you think you do.

Benjamin Spock

❧ ❧ ❧ ❧

WRITING IS NOTHING more than a guided dream.

Jorge Luis Borges

❧ ❧ ❧ ❧

IF YOU THINK education is expensive—try ignorance.

Derek C. Bok

❧ ❧ ❧ ❧

THE GREAT SECRET in life [is] not to open your letters for a fortnight. At the expiration of that period you will find that nearly all of them have answered themselves.

Arthur Binstead

❧ ❧ ❧ ❧

THE CHARM OF HISTORY and its enigmatic lesson consist in the fact that, from age to age, nothing changes and yet everything is completely different.

Aldous Huxley

❧ ❧ ❧ ❧

WEEPING MAY ENDURE for a night, but joy cometh in the morning.

Psalm 30:5 (KJV)

⚜ ⚜ ⚜ ⚜

THE RECIPE FOR perpetual ignorance is: Be satisfied with your opinions and content with your knowledge.

Elbert Hubbard

⚜ ⚜ ⚜ ⚜

IF THERE'S NO MONEY in poetry, neither is there poetry in money.

Robert Graves

⚜ ⚜ ⚜ ⚜

ONE CAN ACQUIRE everything in solitude—except character.

Stendhal

⚜ ⚜ ⚜ ⚜

I DO TO OTHERS what they do to me, only worse.

Jimmy Hoffa

⚜ ⚜ ⚜ ⚜

WE ARE ALL BUT recent leaves on the same old tree of life and if this life has adapted itself to new functions and conditions, it uses the same old basic principles over and over again. There is no real difference between the grass and the man who mows it.

Albert Szent-Györgyi

⚜ ⚜ ⚜ ⚜

ON A JOURNEY ILL,
And over fields all withered, dreams
Go wandering still.

Matsuo Basho

⚜ ⚜ ⚜ ⚜

MAYBE THIS WORLD is another planet's Hell.

Aldous Huxley

⚜ ⚜ ⚜ ⚜

NEVER THINK you've seen the last of anything.

Eudora Welty

⚜ ⚜ ⚜ ⚜

THE PHILOSOPHERS have only interpreted the world in various ways: The point, however, is to change it.

Karl Marx

⚜ ⚜ ⚜ ⚜

THE BASIC TOOL for the manipulation of reality is the manipulation of words. If you can control the meaning of words, you can control the people who must use the words.

Philip K. Dick

⚜ ⚜ ⚜ ⚜

IN THREE WORDS I can sum up everything I've learned about life: It goes on.

Robert Frost

⚜ ⚜ ⚜ ⚜

THE DREAM IS A LITTLE hidden door in the innermost and most secret recesses of the soul, opening into that cosmic night which was psyche long before there was any ego-consciousness, and which will remain psyche no matter how far out ego-consciousness extends.

Carl Jung

❧ ❧ ❧ ❧

I NEVER SAW a mob rush across town to do a good deed.

Wilson Mizner

❧ ❧ ❧ ❧

GIVE ME WHERE TO STAND, and I will move the earth.

Archimedes

❧ ❧ ❧ ❧

TO ACHIEVE GREAT THINGS, we must live as though we were never going to die.

Luc de Clapiers, Marquis de Vauvenargues

❧ ❧ ❧ ❧

WHAT DOES NOT destroy me, makes me stronger.

Friedrich Nietzsche

❧ ❧ ❧ ❧

IT'S GONNA BE a long hard drag, but we'll make it.

Janis Joplin

❧ ❧ ❧ ❧

IT IS MUCH MORE difficult to judge oneself than to judge others. If you succeed in judging yourself rightly, then you are indeed a man of true wisdom.

Antoine de Saint-Exupéry

❧ ❧ ❧ ❧

WE MUST BE the change we wish to see in the world.

Mohandas Gandhi

❧ ❧ ❧ ❧

I CAN'T EVEN SAY I made my own mistake. Really—one has to ask oneself—what dignity is there in that?

Kazuo Ishiguro

❧ ❧ ❧ ❧

AFTER ALL, HUMAN BEINGS are like that: When they are alone they want to be with others, and when they are with others they want to be alone.

Gertrude Stein

❧ ❧ ❧ ❧

I WANT THE WHOLE of Europe to have one currency; it will make trading much easier.

Napoléon Bonaparte

❧ ❧ ❧ ❧

WINNING ISN'T EVERYTHING, but wanting to win is!

Vince Lombardi

❧ ❧ ❧ ❧

HEREIN LIES OUR PROBLEM. If we level that much land to grow rice and whatever, then no other animal could live there except for some insect pest species. Which is very unfortunate.

Steve Irwin

❧ ❧ ❧ ❧

A BORE IS A MAN who, when you ask him how he is, tells you.

Bert Leston Taylor

❧ ❧ ❧ ❧

SHOW ME A thoroughly satisfied man, and I will show you a failure.

Thomas Alva Edison

❧ ❧ ❧ ❧

I STARTED AT THE TOP and worked my way down.

Orson Welles

❧ ❧ ❧ ❧

ALL MUSIC IS FOLK MUSIC. I ain't never heard no horse sing a song.

Louis Armstrong

❧ ❧ ❧ ❧

IF A MAN DOES NOT keep pace with his companions, perhaps it is because he hears a different drummer. Let him step to the music which he hears, however measured or far away.

Henry David Thoreau

❧ ❧ ❧ ❧

CHARM IS THE QUALITY in others that makes us more satisfied with ourselves.

Henri-Frédéric Amiel

❧ ❧ ❧ ❧

GREAT THINGS are not accomplished by those who yield to trends and fads and popular opinion.

Jack Kerouac

❧ ❧ ❧ ❧

THE ONLY abnormality is the incapacity to love.

Anaïs Nin

❧ ❧ ❧ ❧

UNLESS ONE SAYS goodbye to what one loves, and unless one travels to completely new territories, one can expect merely a long wearing away of oneself and an eventual extinction.

Jean Dubuffet

❧ ❧ ❧ ❧

IF THEY CAN get you asking the wrong questions, they don't have to worry about answers.

Thomas Pynchon

❧ ❧ ❧ ❧

GOD ALONE KNOWS the future, but only an historian can alter the past.

Ambrose Bierce

❧ ❧ ❧ ❧

TIME IS A STORM in which we are all lost.

William Carlos Williams

❖ ❖ ❖ ❖

FORMULA FOR SUCCESS: Underpromise and overdeliver.

Tom Peters

❖ ❖ ❖ ❖

I HAVE A SECRET PASSION for mercy… but justice is what keeps happening to people.

Ross MacDonald

❖ ❖ ❖ ❖

MOST MODERN CALENDARS mar the sweet simplicity of our lives by reminding us that each day that passes is the anniversary of some perfectly uninteresting event.

Oscar Wilde

❖ ❖ ❖ ❖

IF YOU BELIEVE THE DOCTORS, nothing is wholesome; if you believe the theologians, nothing is innocent; if you believe the soldiers, nothing is safe.

Robert Gascoyne-Cecil (Lord Salisbury)

❖ ❖ ❖ ❖

WHEN IT IS A QUESTION of money, everybody is of the same religion.

Voltaire

❖ ❖ ❖ ❖

THE LEGAL THEORY IS, that marriage makes the husband and wife one person, and that person is the husband.

Lucretia Mott

EVERY MAN BEARS the whole stamp of the human condition.

Michel de Montaigne

WHAT LIES BEHIND US and what lies before us are small matters to what lies within us.

Anonymous

SILENCE IS DEATH.
And if you say nothing you die,
And if you speak you die.
So speak and die.

Tahar Djaout

WHEN YOU WERE BORN, you cried and the world rejoiced. Live your life so that when you die, the world cries and you rejoice.

White Elk

THERE ARE TWO THINGS over which you have complete dominion, authority, and control—your mind and your mouth.

Molefi Asante

YOU AND I AND EVERYTHING in the universe are part of the infinite flow of the divine love. When we see this, we acknowledge that this same benevolence binds together all creation. When we harmonize with life we come into accord with the part of God that flows through everything. That all life be nurtured and protected is at once our mission and our prayer.

Morihei Ueshiba

❧ ❧ ❧ ❧

NO WISE MAN ever wished to be younger.

Jonathan Swift

❧ ❧ ❧ ❧

THINGS ARE beautiful if you love them.

Jean Anouilh

❧ ❧ ❧ ❧

FORGIVENESS is the key to action and freedom.

Hannah Arendt

❧ ❧ ❧ ❧

SEND THESE, the homeless, tempest toss'd, to me. I lift my lamp beside the golden door.

Emma Lazarus

❧ ❧ ❧ ❧

A WISE MAN knows everything; a shrewd man, everybody.

Anonymous

❧ ❧ ❧ ❧

A WOMAN PAST FORTY should make up her mind to be young—not her face.

Billie Burke

❧ ❧ ❧ ❧

NOTHING IS IMPOSSIBLE for the person who doesn't have to do it.

Weller's Law

❧ ❧ ❧ ❧

WHEN I AM DEAD, I hope it may be said: "His sins were scarlet, but his books were read."

Hilaire Belloc

❧ ❧ ❧ ❧

ONE CAN ONLY FACE in others what one can face in oneself.

James Baldwin

❧ ❧ ❧ ❧

EXPERIENCE SHOWS us that love does not consist in gazing at each other but in looking together in the same direction.

Antoine de Saint-Exupéry

❧ ❧ ❧ ❧

IF WE FIND THE answer to that [why we and the universe exist], it would be the ultimate triumph of human reason—for then we would know the mind of God.

Stephen Hawking

❧ ❧ ❧ ❧

ART IS MEANT to disturb, science reassures.

Georges Braque

✣ ✣ ✣ ✣

THE CEASELESS LABOR of your life is to build the house of death.

Michel de Montaigne

✣ ✣ ✣ ✣

I DO DESIRE we may be better strangers.

William Shakespeare

✣ ✣ ✣ ✣

A BOOKSTORE is one of the only pieces of evidence we have that people are still thinking.

Jerry Seinfeld

✣ ✣ ✣ ✣

THE ROAD UP and the road down are one and the same.

Heraclitus

✣ ✣ ✣ ✣

OUR EXCESSIVE TOLERANCE with regard to suicide is due to the fact that, since the state of mind from which it springs is a general one, we cannot condemn it without condemning ourselves; we are too saturated with it not partly to excuse it.

Émile Durkheim

✣ ✣ ✣ ✣

HAVING THE CRITICS praise you is like having the hangman say you've got a pretty neck.

Eli Wallach

❀ ❀ ❀ ❀

THOUGH BOTH ARE BOUND in the spiral dance, I would rather be a cyborg than a goddess.

Donna Haraway

❀ ❀ ❀ ❀

IF YOU WOULD PERSUADE, you must appeal to interest rather than intellect.

Benjamin Franklin

❀ ❀ ❀ ❀

IT'S A FUNNY THING, the more I practice the luckier I get.

Arnold Palmer

❀ ❀ ❀ ❀

WHEN A DISTINGUISHED but elderly scientist states that something is possible, he is almost certainly right. When he states that something is impossible, he is very probably wrong.

Arthur C. Clarke

❀ ❀ ❀ ❀

IF YOU LISTEN CAREFULLY, you get to hear everything you didn't want to hear in the first place.

Sholem Aleichem

❀ ❀ ❀ ❀

A BOOK IS A MIRROR: When a monkey looks in, no apostle can look out.

Georg Christoph Lichtenberg

⚜ ⚜ ⚜ ⚜

MURDER IS A CRIME. Describing murder is not. Sex is not a crime. Describing sex is.

Gershon Legman

⚜ ⚜ ⚜ ⚜

DOES HISTORY RECORD any case in which the majority was right?

Robert A. Heinlein

⚜ ⚜ ⚜ ⚜

THE STRENGTH OF A MAN'S VIRTUE should not be measured by his special exertions, but by his habitual acts.

Blaise Pascal

⚜ ⚜ ⚜ ⚜

EXPECTING LIFE to treat you well because you are a good person is like expecting an angry bull not to charge because you are a vegetarian.

Shari R. Barr

⚜ ⚜ ⚜ ⚜

THE GREAT PLEASURE of a dog is that you may make a fool of yourself with him and not only will he not scold you, but he will make a fool of himself, too.

Samuel Butler

⚜ ⚜ ⚜ ⚜

THE MOST IMPORTANT fact about Spaceship Earth: An instruction book didn't come with it.

Buckminster Fuller

⚜ ⚜ ⚜ ⚜

DEATH IS NOT EXTINGUISHING the light; it is putting out the lamp because dawn has come.

Rabindranath Tagore

⚜ ⚜ ⚜ ⚜

LIFE IS PAINTING a picture, not doing a sum.

Oliver Wendell Holmes

⚜ ⚜ ⚜ ⚜

THERE ARE 12 HOURS in the day, and above 50 in the night.

Marie de Rabutin-Chantal, Marquise de Sévigné

⚜ ⚜ ⚜ ⚜

THERE IS NO PERFECTION ... this is a broken world and we live with broken hearts and broken lives, but still, that is no alibi for anything. On the contrary, you have to stand up and say hallelujah under those circumstances.

Leonard Cohen

⚜ ⚜ ⚜ ⚜

I AM LOOKING for an honest man.

Diogenes

⚜ ⚜ ⚜ ⚜

WE BECOME NOT a melting pot but a beautiful mosaic—
different people, different beliefs, different yearnings, different
hopes, different dreams.

James Earl "Jimmy" Carter

❧ ❧ ❧ ❧

WHEN I GIVE FOOD to the poor, they call me a saint. When I ask
why the poor have no food, they call me a communist.

Dom Hélder Câmara

❧ ❧ ❧ ❧

UNTIL YOU MAKE PEACE with who you are, you'll never be
content with what you have.

Doris Mortman

❧ ❧ ❧ ❧

DIPLOMACY is to do and say
the nastiest thing in the nicest way.

Isaac Goldberg

❧ ❧ ❧ ❧

THERE'S SOMETHING about death that is comforting. The
thought that you could die tomorrow frees you to appreciate
your life now.

Angelina Jolie

❧ ❧ ❧ ❧

TRUTH is subjectivity.

Søren Kierkegaard

❧ ❧ ❧ ❧

I READ ABOUT AN ESKIMO HUNTER who asked the local missionary priest, "If I did not know about God and sin, would I go to hell?" "No," said the priest, "not if you did not know." "Then why," asked the Eskimo earnestly, "did you tell me?"

Annie Dillard

❖ ❖ ❖ ❖

ALL THAT GLITTERS is not gold.

William Shakespeare

❖ ❖ ❖ ❖

AN IDEA COMES as close to something for nothing as you can get.

Robert Frost

❖ ❖ ❖ ❖

THE ART OF BEING WISE is the art of knowing what to overlook.

William James

❖ ❖ ❖ ❖

SPEECH IS CIVILIZATION itself. The word, even the most contradictory word, preserves contact—it is silence which isolates.

Thomas Mann

❖ ❖ ❖ ❖

A CAMEL IS A HORSE designed by a committee.

Alex Issigonis

❖ ❖ ❖ ❖

WAR DOES NOT determine who is right—only who is left.

Anonymous

❧ ❧ ❧ ❧

DO NOT PUT YOUR FAITH in what statistics say until you have carefully considered what they do not say.

William W. Watt

❧ ❧ ❧ ❧

HOLDING ON TO ANGER is like grasping a hot coal with the intent of throwing it at someone else; you are the one who gets burned.

Buddha

❧ ❧ ❧ ❧

MAKE NO LITTLE PLANS; they have no magic to stir men's blood.

Daniel Burnham

❧ ❧ ❧ ❧

IT IS ONE THING to show a man that he is in error, and another to put him in possession of truth.

John Locke

❧ ❧ ❧ ❧

HONESTY MAY BE the best policy, but it's important to remember that apparently, by elimination, dishonesty is the second best policy.

George Carlin

❧ ❧ ❧ ❧

YOUNG MEN THINK old men are fools; but old men know young men are fools.

George Chapman

⚜ ⚜ ⚜ ⚜

THEY WHO DREAM by day are cognizant of many things that escape those who dream only by night.

Edgar Allan Poe

⚜ ⚜ ⚜ ⚜

GUILT IS THE PLEDGE drive constantly hammering in our heads that keeps us from fully enjoying the show.

Dennis Miller

⚜ ⚜ ⚜ ⚜

DO NOT LOSE HEART! The steeper the road, the faster it rises towards ever-wider horizons.

Pope John Paul II

⚜ ⚜ ⚜ ⚜

LIFE IS BETTER THAN DEATH, I believe, if only because it is less boring, and because it has fresh peaches in it.

Alice Walker

⚜ ⚜ ⚜ ⚜

ALL PROGRESS IS BASED upon a universal innate desire on the part of every organism to live beyond its income.

Samuel Butler

⚜ ⚜ ⚜ ⚜

CYNICISM IS NOT realistic and tough. It's unrealistic and kind of cowardly because it means you don't have to try.

Peggy Noonan

❧ ❧ ❧ ❧

IT SEEMS TO ME that any sensible person must see that violence does not change the world and if it does, then only temporarily.

Martin Scorsese

❧ ❧ ❧ ❧

GIVE ME CONTROL of a nation's money and I care not who makes the laws.

Mayer Amschel Rothschild

❧ ❧ ❧ ❧

A MAN IS NEVER so on trial as in the moment of excessive good fortune.

Lew Wallace

❧ ❧ ❧ ❧

CARELESSNESS ABOUT OUR security is dangerous; carelessness about our freedom is also dangerous.

Adlai Stevenson

❧ ❧ ❧ ❧

FOR A SUCCESSFUL TECHNOLOGY, reality must take precedence over public relations, for nature cannot be fooled.

Richard P. Feynman

❧ ❧ ❧ ❧

AN INTELLECTUAL is someone whose mind watches itself.

Albert Camus

❧ ❧ ❧ ❧

THERE IS NO SUCH THING as an impartial jury because there are no impartial people. There are people that argue on the Web for hours about who their favorite character on *Friends* is.

Jon Stewart

❧ ❧ ❧ ❧

FROM ERROR TO ERROR, one discovers the entire truth.

Sigmund Freud

❧ ❧ ❧ ❧

KNOCK ON THE SKY and listen to the sound.

Zen proverb

❧ ❧ ❧ ❧

I ADORE SIMPLE PLEASURES. They are the last refuge of the complex.

Oscar Wilde

❧ ❧ ❧ ❧

THE DIFFERENCE BETWEEN the almost right word and the right word is really a large matter—'tis the difference between the lightning bug and the lightning.

Mark Twain

❧ ❧ ❧ ❧

IF WE WANT THINGS to stay as they are, things will have to change.

Giuseppe di Lampedusa

❧ ❧ ❧ ❧

DON'T GET MAD; get even.

Joseph P. Kennedy

❧ ❧ ❧ ❧

NOTHING CAN COME out of an artist that is not in the man.

H. L. Mencken

❧ ❧ ❧ ❧

LOVE IS NOT ALL: It is not meat nor drink,
Nor slumber nor a roof against the rain;
Nor yet a floating spar to men that sink.

Edna St. Vincent Millay

❧ ❧ ❧ ❧

IF AT FIRST you don't succeed, try, try again. Then quit. There's no use being a damn fool about it.

W. C. Fields

❧ ❧ ❧ ❧

I AM AN INVISIBLE MAN. . . . I am a man of substance, of flesh and bone, fiber and liquids—and I might even be said to possess a mind. I am invisible, understand, simply because people refuse to see me.

Ralph Ellison

❧ ❧ ❧ ❧

SEE EVERYTHING: Overlook a great deal; correct a little.

Pope John XXIII

❦ ❦ ❦ ❦

GOD MADE INTEGERS, all else is the work of man.

Leopold Kronecker

❦ ❦ ❦ ❦

I KISSED HER. . . . It was like being in church.

James M. Cain

❦ ❦ ❦ ❦

HUMAN NATURE is largely something that has to be overcome.

Rita Rudner

❦ ❦ ❦ ❦

IN HER FIRST PASSION woman loves her lover; in all the others all she loves is love.

George Gordon, Lord Byron

❦ ❦ ❦ ❦

THE FACT THAT SOME geniuses were laughed at does not imply that all who are laughed at are geniuses. They laughed at Columbus, they laughed at Fulton, they laughed at the Wright Brothers. But they also laughed at Bozo the Clown.

Carl Sagan

❦ ❦ ❦ ❦

THERE CAME A TIME when the risk to remain tight in the bud was more painful than the risk it took to blossom.

Anaïs Nin

❧ ❧ ❧ ❧

ONE MIGHT REGARD architecture as history arrested in stone.

A. L. Rowse

❧ ❧ ❧ ❧

I HEAR AND I FORGET; I see and I remember; I do and I understand.

Chinese proverb

❧ ❧ ❧ ❧

YOU GOTTA WHIP up a storm and keep on blowin'.

Sidney Bechet

❧ ❧ ❧ ❧

VICTORY GOES to the player who makes the next-to-last mistake.

Savielly Grigorievitch Tartakower

❧ ❧ ❧ ❧

ALMOST ALL of our relationships begin, and most of them continue, as forms of mutual exploitation, a mental or physical barter, to be terminated when one or both parties run out of goods.

W. H. Auden

❧ ❧ ❧ ❧

I DON'T KNOW WHY we are here, but I'm pretty sure that it is not in order to enjoy ourselves.

Ludwig Wittgenstein

⚜ ⚜ ⚜ ⚜

THE TRUTH THAT MANY PEOPLE never understand, until it is too late, is that the more you try to avoid suffering the more you suffer because insignficant things begin to torture you in proportion to your fear of being hurt.

Thomas Merton

⚜ ⚜ ⚜ ⚜

THE GLORY OF EACH generation is to make its own precedents.

Belva Lockwood

⚜ ⚜ ⚜ ⚜

A CONVENTIONAL ARMY loses if it does not win. The guerrilla wins if he does not lose.

Henry Kissinger

⚜ ⚜ ⚜ ⚜

DOGS ARE NOT OUR whole life, but they make our lives whole.

Roger Caras

⚜ ⚜ ⚜ ⚜

WHERE I LIVE if someone gives you a hug it's from the heart.

Steve Irwin

⚜ ⚜ ⚜ ⚜

ALL THE NEW THINKING is about loss. In this it resembles the old thinking.

Robert Hass

❖ ❖ ❖ ❖

WHAT ONE has to do usually can be done.

Eleanor Roosevelt

❖ ❖ ❖ ❖

I WOULD RATHER be exposed to the inconveniences attending too much liberty than those attending too small a degree of it.

Thomas Jefferson

❖ ❖ ❖ ❖

HOPE IS ITSELF a species of happiness, and, perhaps, the chief happiness which this world affords.

Samuel Johnson

❖ ❖ ❖ ❖

TOO MANY PIECES of music finish too long after the end.

Igor Stravinsky

❖ ❖ ❖ ❖

A BORE IS A FELLOW talking who can change the subject back to his topic of conversation faster than you can change it back to yours.

Laurence J. Peter

❖ ❖ ❖ ❖

TIME WOULD BECOME meaningless if there were too much of it.

Ray Kurzweil

❧ ❧ ❧ ❧

TO RETAIN RESPECT for laws and sausages, one must not watch them in the making.

Otto von Bismarck

❧ ❧ ❧ ❧

BE THE FIRST to say something obvious and achieve immortality.

Marie von Ebner-Eschenbach

❧ ❧ ❧ ❧

TRUE AUDACITY is the trick of knowing how far you can go in going too far.

Jean Cocteau

❧ ❧ ❧ ❧

AN EXCELLENT QUOTATION can annihilate entire pages, indeed an entire book, in that it warns the reader and seems to cry out to him: "Beware, I am the jewel and around me there is lead, pallid, ignominious lead!"

Friedrich Nietzsche

❧ ❧ ❧ ❧

OLD AGE ISN'T SO BAD when you consider the alternative.

Maurice Chevalier

❧ ❧ ❧ ❧

WITH METHOD AND LOGIC one can accomplish anything.

Agatha Christie

❧ ❧ ❧ ❧

I LIKE LARGE PARTIES. They're so intimate. At small parties there isn't any privacy.

F. Scott Fitzgerald

❧ ❧ ❧ ❧

MY FIRST ACT of free will shall be to believe in free will.

William James

❧ ❧ ❧ ❧

IF ALL MY FRIENDS were to jump off a bridge, I wouldn't jump with them, I'd be at the bottom to catch them. Everyone hears what you say. Friends listen to what you say. Best friends listen to what you don't say. We all take different paths in life, but no matter where we go, we take a little of each other everywhere.

Tim McGraw

❧ ❧ ❧ ❧

MY EYES AND MIND keep taking me where my old legs can't keep up.

Zora Neale Hurston

❧ ❧ ❧ ❧

ART IS EITHER plagiarism or revolution.

Paul Gauguin

❧ ❧ ❧ ❧

IF YOU'RE GOING through hell, keep going.

Winston Churchill

⚜ ⚜ ⚜ ⚜

AN AGE IS CALLED DARK, not because the light fails to shine, but because people refuse to see it.

James Michener

⚜ ⚜ ⚜ ⚜

OUR NATURE LIES in movement; complete rest is death.

Blaise Pascal

⚜ ⚜ ⚜ ⚜

AS SCARCE AS TRUTH IS, the supply has always been in excess of the demand.

Josh Billings

⚜ ⚜ ⚜ ⚜

A NIHILIST IS A MAN who does not bow down before any authority, who does not take any principle on faith, whatever reverence that principle may be enshrined in.

Ivan Turgenev

⚜ ⚜ ⚜ ⚜

MAY THE STARS CARRY your sadness away, may the flowers fill your heart with beauty, may hope forever wipe away your tears, and, above all, may silence make you strong.

Chief Dan George

⚜ ⚜ ⚜ ⚜

THE SIGNIFICANCE OF MAN is that he is that part of the universe that asks the question: What is the significance of man? He alone can stand apart imaginatively and, regarding himself and the universe in their eternal aspects, pronounce a judgment: The significance of man is that he is insignificant and is aware of it.

Carl Becker

⚜ ⚜ ⚜ ⚜

YOU GROW UP the day you have your first real laugh—at yourself.

Ethel Barrymore

⚜ ⚜ ⚜ ⚜

I DON'T KNOW the key to success, but the key to failure is trying to please everybody.

Bill Cosby

⚜ ⚜ ⚜ ⚜

[OF MARK TWAIN:] HIS WIFE not only edited his works but edited him.

Van Wyck Brooks

⚜ ⚜ ⚜ ⚜

A HOUSE IS A machine for living.

Charles-Édouard Jeanneret

⚜ ⚜ ⚜ ⚜

IT'S MY RULE never to lose my temper until it would be detrimental to keep it.

Sean O'Casey

❧ ❧ ❧ ❧

OF THE BILLIONAIRES I have known, money just brings out the basic traits in them. If they were jerks before they had money, they are simply jerks with a billion dollars.

Warren Buffett

❧ ❧ ❧ ❧

THE ENGLISH PUBLIC, as a mass, takes no interest in a work of art until it is told that the work in question is immoral.

Oscar Wilde

❧ ❧ ❧ ❧

YOU WILL NEVER "find" time for anything. If you want time you must make it.

Charles Buxton

❧ ❧ ❧ ❧

THE DIFFICULT IS what takes a little time; the impossible is what takes a little longer.

Fridtjof Nansen

❧ ❧ ❧ ❧

COURAGE IS THE LADDER on which all other virtues mount.

Clare Boothe Luce

❧ ❧ ❧ ❧

SECOND TO AGRICULTURE, humbug is the biggest industry of our age.

Alfred Nobel

⚜ ⚜ ⚜ ⚜

MOST PEOPLE CONSIDER a glass as half empty or half full. I look at it as too big.

George Carlin

⚜ ⚜ ⚜ ⚜

THE BEST THING to hold onto in life is each other.

Audrey Hepburn

⚜ ⚜ ⚜ ⚜

EDUCATION IS WHEN you read the fine print; experience is what you get when you don't.

Pete Seeger

⚜ ⚜ ⚜ ⚜

THIS CEREMONY IS HELD in the depth of winter. But, by the words we speak and the faces we show the world, we force the spring.

Bill Clinton

⚜ ⚜ ⚜ ⚜

SOME FOLKS ARE WISE and some are otherwise.

Tobias Smollett

⚜ ⚜ ⚜ ⚜

I AM AS FRUSTRATED with society as a pyromaniac in a petrified forest.

A. Whitney Brown

❧ ❧ ❧ ❧

ANALYSIS KILLS SPONTANEITY. The grain once ground into flour germinates no more.

Henri-Frédéric Amiel

❧ ❧ ❧ ❧

NO REVENGE is more honorable than the one not taken.

Spanish proverb

❧ ❧ ❧ ❧

GOD ASKS NO MAN whether he will accept life. That is not the choice. You must take it. The only choice is how.

Henry Ward Beecher

❧ ❧ ❧ ❧

NOW I HAVE COME to believe that the whole world is an enigma, a harmless enigma that is made terrible by our own mad attempt to interpret it as though it had an underlying truth.

Umberto Eco

❧ ❧ ❧ ❧

TO APPRECIATE NONSENSE requires a serious interest in life.

Gelett Burgess

❧ ❧ ❧ ❧

SCIENCE WITHOUT RELIGION is lame; religion without science is blind.

Albert Einstein

❧ ❧ ❧ ❧

I WAS THE VICTIM of a series of accidents, as are we all.

Kurt Vonnegut

❧ ❧ ❧ ❧

NO MAN HAS a good enough memory to be a successful liar.

Abraham Lincoln

❧ ❧ ❧ ❧

TRUE GENEROSITY toward the future consists in giving everything to the present.

Albert Camus

❧ ❧ ❧ ❧

THREE PASSIONS, simple but overwhelmingly strong, have governed my life: the longing for love, the search for knowledge, and unbearable pity for the suffering of mankind.

Bertrand Russell

❧ ❧ ❧ ❧

YOU CAN TURN painful situations around through laughter. If you can find humor in anything—even poverty—you can survive it.

Bill Cosby

❧ ❧ ❧ ❧

LIFE'S TRAGEDY is that we get old too soon and wise too late.

Benjamin Franklin

❧ ❧ ❧ ❧

NO RACE CAN PROSPER till it learns that there is as much dignity in tilling a field as in writing a poem.

Booker T. Washington

❧ ❧ ❧ ❧

IT IS A COMMON EXPERIENCE that a problem difficult at night is resolved in the morning after the committee of sleep has worked on it.

John Steinbeck

❧ ❧ ❧ ❧

EDUCATION IS A METHOD whereby one acquires a higher grade of prejudices.

Laurence J. Peter

❧ ❧ ❧ ❧

THE RESPECT THAT IS only bought by gold is not worth much.

Frances E. W. Harper

❧ ❧ ❧ ❧

I WAS BROUGHT UP to believe that the only thing worth doing was to add to the sum of accurate information in this world.

Margaret Mead

❧ ❧ ❧ ❧

THERE IS A CRACK in everything, that is how the light gets in.

Leonard Cohen

❧ ❧ ❧ ❧

FANATICISM CONSISTS in redoubling your effort when you have forgotten your aim.

George Santayana

❧ ❧ ❧ ❧

CONSCIENCE IS THE INNER voice that warns us somebody may be looking.

H. L. Mencken

❧ ❧ ❧ ❧

ONE OF THE SOURCES of pride in being a human being is the ability to bear present frustrations in the interests of longer purposes.

Helen Merrell Lynd

❧ ❧ ❧ ❧

COMMIT A CRIME and the world is made of glass.

Ralph Waldo Emerson

❧ ❧ ❧ ❧

NO ONE LIGHTS a lamp and puts it in a place where it will be hidden, or under a bowl. Instead, he puts it on its stand, so that those who come in may see the light.

Luke 11:33 (NIV)

❧ ❧ ❧ ❧

A BILL IS COMING in that I fear America is not prepared to pay.

James Baldwin

❧ ❧ ❧ ❧

THE PAST SHOULD be a springboard, not a hammock.

Ivern Ball

❧ ❧ ❧ ❧

OLD HIPPIES DON'T DIE, they just lie low until the laughter stops and their time comes 'round again.

Joseph Gallivan

❧ ❧ ❧ ❧

TRULY IT HAS BEEN SAID, that to a clear eye the smallest fact is a window through which the Infinite may be seen.

Thomas Henry Huxley

❧ ❧ ❧ ❧

HAPPINESS IS AN IMAGINARY condition, formerly often attributed by the living to the dead, now usually attributed by adults to children, and by children to adults.

Thomas Szasz

❧ ❧ ❧ ❧

PITY THE CRIMINAL all you like, but don't call evil good.

Fyodor Dostoyevsky

❧ ❧ ❧ ❧

IT IS BETTER to be quotable than honest.

Tom Stoppard

❧ ❧ ❧ ❧

SCRATCH A DOG and you'll find a permanent job.

Franklin P. Jones

❧ ❧ ❧ ❧

THE HUMAN RACE has improved everything except the human race.

Adlai Stevenson

❧ ❧ ❧ ❧

EVERY CHILD IS AN ARTIST. The problem is how to remain an artist once he grows up.

Pablo Picasso

❧ ❧ ❧ ❧

THE SPIRIT, THE WILL TO WIN, and the will to excel are the things that endure. These qualities are so much more important than the events that occur.

Vince Lombardi

❧ ❧ ❧ ❧

NO MATTER HOW LONELY you get or how many birth announcements you receive, the trick is not to get frightened. There's nothing wrong with being alone.

Wendy Wasserstein

❧ ❧ ❧ ❧

IT IS COWARDICE to perceive what is right but not to do it.

Confucius

❧ ❧ ❧ ❧

FLESH WAS THE REASON why oil painting was invented.

Willem de Kooning

❧ ❧ ❧ ❧

NO SNOWFLAKE EVER falls in the wrong place.

Zen proverb

❧ ❧ ❧ ❧

IF I'D KNOWN I was gonna live this long [100 years], I'd have taken better care of myself.

Eubie Blake

❧ ❧ ❧ ❧

OUR CREDULITY IS GREATEST concerning the things we know least about. And since we know least about ourselves, we are ready to believe all that is said about us. Hence the mysterious power of both flattery and calumny.

Eric Hoffer

❧ ❧ ❧ ❧

THE END CANNOT justify the means, for the simple and obvious reason that the means employed determine the nature of the ends produced.

Aldous Huxley

❧ ❧ ❧ ❧

BEGIN CHALLENGING YOUR own assumptions. Your assumptions are your windows on the world. Scrub them off every once in awhile, or the light won't come in.

Alan Alda

✧ ✧ ✧ ✧

COMMON SENSE is the best sense I know of.

Philip Dormer Stanhope (Lord Chesterfield)

✧ ✧ ✧ ✧

THE ONLY REASON for time is so that everything doesn't happen all at once.

Albert Einstein

✧ ✧ ✧ ✧

IF FIFTY MILLION PEOPLE say a foolish thing, it is still a foolish thing.

Anatole France

✧ ✧ ✧ ✧

WHAT EXACTLY IS SUCCESS? For me it is to be found not in applause, but in the satisfaction of feeling that one is realizing one's ideal.

Anna Pavlova

✧ ✧ ✧ ✧

A LIE CAN BE HALFWAY 'round the world before the truth has got its boots on.

Anonymous

✧ ✧ ✧ ✧

DON'T EVER SLAM THE DOOR; you might want to go back.

Don Herold

❖ ❖ ❖ ❖

WHAT IS MAN IN NATURE? A nothing compared to the infinite, an everything compared to nothing, a midpoint between nothing and everything.

Blaise Pascal

❖ ❖ ❖ ❖

WHERE THOU ART—that is Home.

Emily Dickinson

❖ ❖ ❖ ❖

TELEVISION is chewing gum for the eyes.

John Mason Brown

❖ ❖ ❖ ❖

A VEGETABLE GARDEN in the beginning looks so promising and then after all little by little it grows nothing but vegetables, nothing, nothing but vegetables.

Gertrude Stein

❖ ❖ ❖ ❖

GENIUS ALL OVER the world stands hand in hand, and one shock of recognition runs the whole circle round.

Herman Melville

❖ ❖ ❖ ❖

BEWARE OF ALL enterprises that require new clothes.

Henry David Thoreau

❧ ❧ ❧ ❧

KEEP TRUE to the dreams of thy youth.

Friedrich von Schiller

❧ ❧ ❧ ❧

HIS SOUL SWOONED slowly as he heard the snow falling faintly through the universe and faintly falling, like the descent of their last end, upon all the living and the dead.

James Joyce

❧ ❧ ❧ ❧

EVERYTHING has been figured out, except how to live.

Jean-Paul Sartre

❧ ❧ ❧ ❧

HISTORY IS NOTHING more than a tableau of crimes and misfortunes.

Voltaire

❧ ❧ ❧ ❧

THERE IS SUFFERING in life, and there are defeats. No one can avoid them. But it's better to lose some of the battles in the struggles for your dreams than to be defeated without ever knowing what you're fighting for.

Paulo Coelho

❧ ❧ ❧ ❧

I BELIEVE THAT EVERYONE is the keeper of a dream—and by tuning into one another's secret hopes, we can become better friends, better partners, better parents, and better lovers.

Oprah Winfrey

❧ ❧ ❧ ❧

THE LIST IS AN ABSOLUTE GOOD. The list is life. All around its cramped margins lies the gulf.

Thomas Keneally

❧ ❧ ❧ ❧

LIFE IS A JOKE that's just begun.

W. S. Gilbert

❧ ❧ ❧ ❧

PEOPLE DON'T EVER seem to realize that doing what's right is no guarantee against misfortune.

William McFee

❧ ❧ ❧ ❧

A WORK THAT ASPIRES, however humbly, to the condition of art should carry its justification in every line.

Joseph Conrad

❧ ❧ ❧ ❧

A CAREER IS BORN in public—talent in privacy.

Marilyn Monroe

❧ ❧ ❧ ❧

LONG IS THE ROAD from conception to completion.

Jean-Baptiste Poquelin Molière

❧ ❧ ❧ ❧

SO LONG AS MAN remains free he strives for nothing so incessantly and so painfully as to find someone to worship.

Fyodor Dostoyevsky

❧ ❧ ❧ ❧

A GOOD NOVEL tells us the truth about its hero, but a bad novel tells us the truth about its author.

G. K. Chesterton

❧ ❧ ❧ ❧

THE ABSENT are always wrong.

French proverb

❧ ❧ ❧ ❧

I MAY NOT HAVE GONE where I intended to go, but I think I have ended up where I needed to be.

Douglas Adams

❧ ❧ ❧ ❧

POLITICS IN THE MIDDLE of things concerning the imagination are like a pistol shot in the middle of a concert.

Stendhal

❧ ❧ ❧ ❧

HE WHO ASKS A QUESTION is a fool for five minutes; he who does not ask a question remains a fool forever.

Chinese proverb

⚜ ⚜ ⚜ ⚜

WHAT A GOOD THING Adam had—when he said a good thing he knew nobody had said it before.

Mark Twain

⚜ ⚜ ⚜ ⚜

LOOK AT EVERYTHING always as though you were seeing it either for the first or last time: Thus is your time on earth filled with glory.

Betty Smith

⚜ ⚜ ⚜ ⚜

A HUNGRY MAN is not a free man.

Adlai Stevenson

⚜ ⚜ ⚜ ⚜

THE INTERNET IS JUST A WORLD passing around notes in a classroom.

Jon Stewart

⚜ ⚜ ⚜ ⚜

ART IS A MICROSCOPE which the artist fixes on the mysteries of his soul, and shows to people these mysteries which are common to all.

Leo Tolstoy

⚜ ⚜ ⚜ ⚜

DIE KNOWING something. You are not here long.

Walker Evans

❧ ❧ ❧ ❧

VIEWED FROM THE DISTANCE of the moon, the astonishing thing about the earth is that it is alive.... Aloft, floating free beneath the moist, gleaming membrane of bright blue sky, is the rising earth, the only exuberant thing in this part of the cosmos.... It has the organized, self-contained look of a live creature, full of information, marvelously skilled in handling the sun.

Lewis Thomas

❧ ❧ ❧ ❧

AGE HAS a good mind and sorry shanks.

Pietro Aretino

❧ ❧ ❧ ❧

ANXIETY IS THE INTEREST paid on trouble before it is due.

William Ralph Inge

❧ ❧ ❧ ❧

THERE IS NO SOLITUDE in the world like that of the big city.

Kathleen Norris

❧ ❧ ❧ ❧

I LEAVE before being left. I decide.

Brigitte Bardot

❧ ❧ ❧ ❧

IT'S ONLY THOSE who do nothing that make no mistakes, I suppose.

Joseph Conrad

⚜ ⚜ ⚜ ⚜

WHO CAN refute a sneer?

William Paley

⚜ ⚜ ⚜ ⚜

I GO ABOUT LOOKING at horses and cattle. They eat grass, make love, work when they have to, bear their young. I am sick with envy of them.

Sherwood Anderson

⚜ ⚜ ⚜ ⚜

BABIES ARE SUCH a nice way to start people.

Don Herold

⚜ ⚜ ⚜ ⚜

WHO WERE THE FOOLS who spread the story that brute force cannot kill ideas? Nothing is easier. And once they are dead they are no more than corpses.

Simone Weil

⚜ ⚜ ⚜ ⚜

THE HISTORIAN, essentially, wants more documents than he can really use; the dramatist only wants more liberties than he can really take.

Henry James

⚜ ⚜ ⚜ ⚜

ALL HUMAN KNOWLEDGE is precious whether or not it serves the slightest human use.

A. E. Housman

⚜ ⚜ ⚜ ⚜

EVERYTHING THAT IRRITATES us about others can lead us to an understanding of ourselves.

Carl Jung

⚜ ⚜ ⚜ ⚜

THE BEST ARGUMENT against democracy is a five-minute conversation with the average voter.

Winston Churchill

⚜ ⚜ ⚜ ⚜

I WASN'T AFRAID TO FAIL. Something good always comes out of failure.

Anne Baxter

⚜ ⚜ ⚜ ⚜

THERE ARE BUT three events which concern man: birth, life, and death. They are unconscious of their birth, they suffer when they die, and they neglect to live.

Jean de La Bruyère

⚜ ⚜ ⚜ ⚜

AT TIMES, our own light goes out and is rekindled by a spark from another person.

Dr. Albert Schweitzer

⚜ ⚜ ⚜ ⚜

IT HELPS IF the hitter thinks you're a little crazy.

Nolan Ryan

✠ ✠ ✠ ✠

TRUE COURAGE is facing danger when you are afraid.

L. Frank Baum

✠ ✠ ✠ ✠

HOW MANY OF OUR daydreams would darken into nightmares, were there any danger of their coming true!

Logan Pearsall Smith

✠ ✠ ✠ ✠

AS FOR BEING A GENERAL, well, at the age of four with paper hats and wooden swords we're all generals. Only some of us never grow out of it.

Peter Ustinov

✠ ✠ ✠ ✠

I BELIEVE THAT A SCIENTIST looking at non-scientific problems is just as dumb as the next guy.

Richard P. Feynman

✠ ✠ ✠ ✠

THE ONLY PERSON you should ever compete with is yourself. You can't hope for a fairer match.

Todd Ruthman

✠ ✠ ✠ ✠

CHILDHOOD IS SHORT; maturity is forever.

Bill Watterson

❧ ❧ ❧ ❧

I THINK COMPUTER VIRUSES should count as life. I think it says something about human nature that the only form of life we have created so far is purely destructive. We've created life in our own image.

Stephen Hawking

❧ ❧ ❧ ❧

BETTER BE QUARRELLING than lonesome.

Irish proverb

❧ ❧ ❧ ❧

I NEVER SAW A WILD thing sorry for itself.

D. H. Lawrence

❧ ❧ ❧ ❧

YOU MISS 100 PERCENT of the shots you never take.

Wayne Gretzky

❧ ❧ ❧ ❧

I DO NOT THINK that the measure of a civilization is how tall its buildings of concrete are, but rather how well its people have learned to relate to their environment and fellow man.

Sun Bear

❧ ❧ ❧ ❧

IN DREAMS BEGINS responsibility.

William Butler Yeats

❧ ❧ ❧ ❧

FINISH EVERY DAY and be done with it. You have done what you could; some blunders and absurdities crept in; forget them as soon as you can. Tomorrow is a new day. You shall begin it well and serenely, and with too high a spirit to be cumbered with your old nonsense.

Ralph Waldo Emerson

❧ ❧ ❧ ❧

I LEARN BY GOING where I have to go.

Theodore Roethke

❧ ❧ ❧ ❧

YOU CAN'T BASE your life on other people's expectations.

Stevie Wonder

❧ ❧ ❧ ❧

THERE IS NOTHING so absurd but some philosopher has said it.

Marcus Tullius Cicero

❧ ❧ ❧ ❧

THE FUTURE DESTINY of the child is always the work of the mother.

Napoléon Bonaparte

❧ ❧ ❧ ❧

THE SHORTEST answer is doing.

English proverb

❧ ❧ ❧ ❧

TO CHERISH WHAT REMAINS of the Earth and to foster its renewal is our only legtimate hope of survival.

Wendell Berry

❧ ❧ ❧ ❧

WE LIVE, as we dream—alone.

Joseph Conrad

❧ ❧ ❧ ❧

AS RAIN FALLS EQUALLY on the just and the unjust, do not burden your heart with judgments but rain your kindness equally on all.

Buddha

❧ ❧ ❧ ❧

MODERN MAN OFTEN talks of the battle with nature, forgetting that if he ever won the battle, he would be on the losing side.

Ernst F. Schumacher

❧ ❧ ❧ ❧

DREAMING IS AN ACT of pure imagination, attesting in all men a creative power, which if it were available in waking, would make every man a Dante or Shakespeare.

H. F. Hedge

❧ ❧ ❧ ❧

IN THEORY, theory and practice are the same. In practice, they are not.

Albert Einstein

⚜ ⚜ ⚜ ⚜

WHAT WISDOM can you find that is greater than kindness?

Jean-Jacques Rousseau

⚜ ⚜ ⚜ ⚜

I AM EASILY satisfied with the very best.

Winston Churchill

⚜ ⚜ ⚜ ⚜

OUR BODY IS A MACHINE for living. It is organized for that, it is its nature. Let life go on in it unhindered and let it defend itself, it will do more than if you paralyze it by encumbering it with remedies.

Leo Tolstoy

⚜ ⚜ ⚜ ⚜

NOTHING CAN DIM the light which shines from within.

Maya Angelou

⚜ ⚜ ⚜ ⚜

A LIBRARY, TO MODIFY the famous metaphor of Socrates, should be the delivery room for the birth of ideas—a place where history comes to life.

Norman Cousins

⚜ ⚜ ⚜ ⚜

JOURNALISM IS THE ABILITY to meet the challenge of filling space.

Rebecca West

❀ ❀ ❀ ❀

IN LITERARY HISTORY, generation follows generation in a rage.

Annie Dillard

❀ ❀ ❀ ❀

A SUCCESSFUL BOOK is not made of what is *in* it, but of what is left *out* of it.

Mark Twain

❀ ❀ ❀ ❀

IF YOU DO A GOOD JOB for others, you heal yourself at the same time, because a dose of joy is a spiritual cure.

Dietrich Bonhoeffer

❀ ❀ ❀ ❀

PEOPLE NEED A SACRED NARRATIVE. They must have a sense of larger purpose, in one form or another, however intellectual-ized. They will find a way to keep ancestral spirits alive.

Edward O. Wilson

❀ ❀ ❀ ❀

SAFEGUARDING THE RIGHTS of others is the most noble and beautiful end of a human being.

Kahlil Gibran

❀ ❀ ❀ ❀

TACT IS THE intelligence of the heart.

Anonymous

❧ ❧ ❧ ❧

FORGIVE YOUR ENEMIES, but never forget their names.

John F. Kennedy

❧ ❧ ❧ ❧

I HAVE NOT A WORD to say against contented people, so long as they keep quiet. But do not, for goodness sake, let them go strutting about, as they are so fond of doing, crying out that they are the true models for the whole species.

Jerome K. Jerome

❧ ❧ ❧ ❧

SOMETIMES YOU CAN'T realize you're in a bad mood until another person enters your orbit.

Douglas Coupland

❧ ❧ ❧ ❧

WE NEVER LIVE, but we are always in the expectation of living.

Voltaire

❧ ❧ ❧ ❧

BUT I HAVE PROMISES to keep, and miles to go before I sleep, and miles to go before I sleep.

Robert Frost

❧ ❧ ❧ ❧

I SUPPOSE IT IS TEMPTING, if the only tool you have is a hammer, to treat everything as if it were a nail.... [Some] choose to work as best they can with important problems (problem-centering) rather than restricting themselves to doing only that which they can do elegantly with the techniques already available (method-centering).

Abraham Maslow

❦ ❦ ❦ ❦

HAPPINESS IS NOT A GOAL; it is a by-product.

Eleanor Roosevelt

❦ ❦ ❦ ❦

WAR IS THE UNFOLDING of miscalculations.

Barbara Tuchman

❦ ❦ ❦ ❦

ALL OUR INTERIOR world is reality—and perhaps more so than our apparent world.

Marc Chagall

❦ ❦ ❦ ❦

HAPPINESS COMES more from loving than being loved; and often when an affection seems wounded it is only our vanity bleeding. To love, and to be hurt often, and to love again—this is the brave and happy life.

J. E. Buckrose

❦ ❦ ❦ ❦

THE OPPOSITE OF LOVE is not hate, it's indifference.

Elie Wiesel

⚜ ⚜ ⚜ ⚜

IF WE COULD SELL our experiences for what they cost us, we'd all be millionaires.

Abigail Van Buren

⚜ ⚜ ⚜ ⚜

WHEN I AM WORKING on a problem, I never think about beauty. I only think about how to solve the problem. But when I have finished, if the solution is not beautiful, I know it is wrong.

Buckminster Fuller

⚜ ⚜ ⚜ ⚜

THE TIME TO STOP a revolution is at the beginning, not the end.

Adlai Stevenson

⚜ ⚜ ⚜ ⚜

YOU KNOW WHAT charm is: a way of getting the answer "yes" without having asked any clear question.

Albert Camus

⚜ ⚜ ⚜ ⚜

THERE IS ONE WAY to find out if a man is honest—ask him. If he says "yes," you know he is crooked.

Groucho Marx

⚜ ⚜ ⚜ ⚜

IN A HIERARCHY every employee tends to rise to his level of incompetence.

Laurence J. Peter

❧ ❧ ❧ ❧

WE CAN'T RELY on anyone but ourselves to define our existence, to shape the image of ourselves.

Spike Lee

❧ ❧ ❧ ❧

SCIENCE IS A WAY of thinking much more than it is a body of knowledge.

Carl Sagan

❧ ❧ ❧ ❧

ONE DAY, SOMEONE SHOWED me a glass of water that was half full. And he said, "Is it half full or half empty?" So I drank the water. No more problem.

Alejandro Jodorowsky

❧ ❧ ❧ ❧

I SEE A SONG as the ashes of existence.

Leonard Cohen

❧ ❧ ❧ ❧

LET PEOPLE HOLD on to these: Manifest plainness, Embrace simplicity, Reduce selfishness, Have few desires.

Lao Tzu

❧ ❧ ❧ ❧

THE POWER OF ACCURATE observation is commonly called cynicism by those who don't have it.

George Bernard Shaw

❧ ❧ ❧ ❧

UNTIL ONE HAS LOVED an animal, a part of one's soul remains unawakened.

Anatole France

❧ ❧ ❧ ❧

PHOTOGRAPHY IS TRUTH. The cinema is truth 24 times per second.

Jean-Luc Godard

❧ ❧ ❧ ❧

I AM TWO FOOLS, I know,
For loving and for saying so.

John Donne

❧ ❧ ❧ ❧

ACTING IS THE MOST MINOR of gifts and not a very high-class way to earn a living. After all, Shirley Temple could do it at the age of four.

Katharine Hepburn

❧ ❧ ❧ ❧

AUTOBIOGRAPHY IS AN UNRIVALED vehicle for telling the truth about other people.

Philip Guedalla

❧ ❧ ❧ ❧

A MAN'S WORST DIFFICULTIES begin when he is able to do as he likes.

Thomas Henry Huxley

❖ ❖ ❖ ❖

COLLEGE IS SOMETHING you complete. Life is something you experience.

Jon Stewart

❖ ❖ ❖ ❖

LIFE IS TRYING things to see if they work.

Ray Bradbury

❖ ❖ ❖ ❖

JUNK IS THE IDEAL PRODUCT... the ultimate merchandise. No sales talk necessary. The client will crawl through a sewer and beg to buy.

William S. Burroughs

❖ ❖ ❖ ❖

THE REAL DANGER is not that computers will begin to think like men, but that men will begin to think like computers.

Sydney J. Harris

❖ ❖ ❖ ❖

IN ALL RECORDED HISTORY there has not been one economist who has had to worry about where the next meal would come from.

Peter Drucker

❖ ❖ ❖ ❖

ALL THE WORLD'S A STAGE, and all the men and women merely players.

William Shakespeare

�֍ ✤ ✤ ✤

BETWEEN SAYING AND DOING many a pair of shoes is worn out.

Italian proverb

✤ ✤ ✤ ✤

ABSENCES ARE A GOOD influence in love and keep it bright and delicate.

Robert Louis Stevenson

✤ ✤ ✤ ✤

THE GREAT BUSINESS of life is to be, to do, to do without, and to depart.

John Morley

✤ ✤ ✤ ✤

IF A MAN COULD PASS through Paradise in a dream, and have a flower presented to him as a pledge that his soul had really been there, and if he found that flower in his hand when he awoke—Ay! and what then?

Samuel Taylor Coleridge

✤ ✤ ✤ ✤

WE HAVE TO BELIEVE in free will. We've got no other choice.

Isaac Bashevis Singer

✤ ✤ ✤ ✤

AS FAR AS WE CAN DISCERN, the sole purpose of human existence is to kindle a light of meaning in the darkness of mere being.

Carl Jung

🌼 🌼 🌼 🌼

WE WERE BORN TO STRUGGLE, to face the challenges of our lifetime and, ultimately, to evolve to a higher consciousness.

Quincy Jones

🌼 🌼 🌼 🌼

WHAT CAN BE HOPED for which is not believed?

St. Augustine

🌼 🌼 🌼 🌼

ONCE YOU ELIMINATE the impossible, whatever remains, no matter how improbable, must be the truth.

Sir Arthur Conan Doyle

🌼 🌼 🌼 🌼

BIG BROTHER is watching you.

George Orwell

🌼 🌼 🌼 🌼

REMEMBER, REMEMBER, this is now, and now, and now. Live it, feel it, cling to it. I want to become acutely aware of all I've taken for granted.

Sylvia Plath

🌼 🌼 🌼 🌼

FAITH IS THE CENTERPIECE of a connected life. It allows us to live by the grace of invisible strands. It is a belief in a wisdom superior to our own. Faith becomes a teacher in the absence of fact.

Terry Tempest Williams

🔹 🔹 🔹 🔹

DREAMING PERMITS each and every one of us to be quietly and safely insane every night of our lives.

William Dement

🔹 🔹 🔹 🔹

MY DEFINITION of a free society is a society where it is safe to be unpopular.

Adlai Stevenson

🔹 🔹 🔹 🔹

KNOW YOURSELF. Don't accept your dog's admiration as conclusive evidence that you are wonderful.

Ann Landers

🔹 🔹 🔹 🔹

ONCE A NEWSPAPER touches a story, the facts are lost forever, even to the protagonists.

Norman Mailer

🔹 🔹 🔹 🔹

TO ME, OLD AGE IS ALWAYS fifteen years older than I am.

Bernard M. Baruch

🔹 🔹 🔹 🔹

THE OPPOSITE OF A CORRECT statement is a false statement. But the opposite of a profound truth may well be another profound truth.

Niels Bohr

❀ ❀ ❀ ❀

HUMAN LIFE IS EVERYWHERE a state in which much is to be endured, and little to be enjoyed.

Samuel Johnson

❀ ❀ ❀ ❀

ANGER IS NEVER WITHOUT reason, but seldom with a good one.

Benjamin Franklin

❀ ❀ ❀ ❀

THE DIFFERENCE BETWEEN stupidity and genius is that genius has its limits.

Albert Einstein

❀ ❀ ❀ ❀

THE FOOLISH NEITHER forgive nor forget. The naïve forgive and forget. The wise forgive but do not forget.

Thomas Szasz

❀ ❀ ❀ ❀

YOU MUST NOT CHANGE one thing, one pebble, one grain of sand, until you know what good and evil will follow on that act.

Ursula K. Le Guin

❀ ❀ ❀ ❀

THE BEST WAY TO PREDICT the future is to invent it.

Alan Kay

❖ ❖ ❖ ❖

THE PUBLIC IS WONDERFULLY tolerant. It forgives everything except genius.

Oscar Wilde

❖ ❖ ❖ ❖

THERE IS JUST ONE THING I can promise you about the outer-space program: Your tax dollar will go farther.

Wernher von Braun

❖ ❖ ❖ ❖

NEVER GO TO BED MAD. Stay up and fight.

Phyllis Diller

❖ ❖ ❖ ❖

LIFE IS JUST A SHORT WALK from the cradle to the grave, and it sure behooves us to be kind to one another along the way.

Alice Childress

❖ ❖ ❖ ❖

GOD IS IN the details.

Aby Warburg

❖ ❖ ❖ ❖

THE TRICK IS IN WHAT one emphasizes. We either make ourselves miserable, or we make ourselves strong. The amount of work is the same.

Carlos Castaneda

❖ ❖ ❖ ❖

WHAT WE THINK we become.

Buddha

❖ ❖ ❖ ❖

ANYONE WHO IS CAPABLE of getting themselves made President should on no account be allowed to do the job.

Douglas Adams

❖ ❖ ❖ ❖

PASSIONATE HATRED can give meaning and purpose to an empty life.

Eric Hoffer

❖ ❖ ❖ ❖

EXPOSE YOURSELF to your deepest fear; after that, fear has no power, and the fear of freedom shrinks and vanishes. You are free.

Jim Morrison

❖ ❖ ❖ ❖

IN ANY CONTEST between power and patience, bet on patience.

W. B. Prescott

❖ ❖ ❖ ❖

ARE WE having fun yet?

Bill Griffith

⚜ ⚜ ⚜ ⚜

HE HAS ACHIEVED SUCCESS who has lived well, laughed often and loved much; who has enjoyed the trust of pure women, the respect of intelligent men and the love of little children; who has filled his niche and accomplished his task; who has left the world better than he found it, whether by an improved poppy, a perfect poem, or a rescued soul; who has never lacked appreciation of earth's beauty or failed to express it; who has always looked for the best in others and given them the best he had; whose life was an inspiration; whose memory is a benediction.

Bessie Anderson Stanley

⚜ ⚜ ⚜ ⚜

MATURITY IS THE CAPACITY to endure uncertainty.

John Finley

⚜ ⚜ ⚜ ⚜

IT AIN'T OVER 'til it's over.

Yogi Berra

⚜ ⚜ ⚜ ⚜

HOW CAN WEALTH persuade poverty to use its political freedom to keep wealth in power? Here lies the whole art of Conservative politics in the twentieth century.

Aneurin Bevan

⚜ ⚜ ⚜ ⚜

TO ACCOMPLISH GREAT things we must not only act, but also dream; not only plan, but also believe.

Anatole France

🙙 🙙 🙙 🙙

IF YOU CAN DREAM IT, you can do it.

Walt Disney

🙙 🙙 🙙 🙙

THE ONLY WAY 'round is through.

Robert Frost

🙙 🙙 🙙 🙙

GROWN MEN CAN LEARN from very little children, for the hearts of little children are pure. Therefore, the Great Spirit may show to them many things which older people miss.

Black Elk

🙙 🙙 🙙 🙙

HER SECRET? It is every artist's secret . . . passion. That is all. It is an open secret, and perfectly safe. Like heroism, it is inimitable in cheap materials.

Willa Cather

🙙 🙙 🙙 🙙

"WHY NOT?" IS A SLOGAN for an interesting life.

Mason Cooley

🙙 🙙 🙙 🙙

THAT EVERYONE SHALL exert himself in that state of life in which he is placed, to practice true humanity toward his fellow men, on that depends the future of mankind.

Dr. Albert Schweitzer

⚜ ⚜ ⚜ ⚜

ONE WRITES ONLY HALF the book; the other half is with the reader.

Joseph Conrad

⚜ ⚜ ⚜ ⚜

THERE IS FAR TOO MUCH law for those who can afford it and far too little for those who cannot.

Derek C. Bok

⚜ ⚜ ⚜ ⚜

IF WHAT YOU HAVE DONE yesterday still looks big to you, you haven't done much today.

Mikhail Gorbachev

⚜ ⚜ ⚜ ⚜

THE MOST POTENT weapon in the hands of the oppressor is the mind of the oppressed.

Stephen Biko

⚜ ⚜ ⚜ ⚜

THERE ARE SOME people so addicted to exaggeration that they can't tell the truth without lying.

Josh Billings

⚜ ⚜ ⚜ ⚜

INTEGRITY WITHOUT KNOWLEDGE is weak and useless, and knowledge without integrity is dangerous and dreadful.

Samuel Johnson

❧ ❧ ❧ ❧

NOT THAT THE STORY need be long, but it will take a long while to make it short.

Henry David Thoreau

❧ ❧ ❧ ❧

THE VOICE OF PASSION is better than the voice of reason. The passionless cannot change history.

Czeslaw Milosz

❧ ❧ ❧ ❧

BUILDINGS should be good neighbors.

Paul Thiry

❧ ❧ ❧ ❧

PARENTS CAN ONLY GIVE good advice or put them on the right paths, but the final forming of a person's character lies in their own hands.

Anne Frank

❧ ❧ ❧ ❧

THE PURPOSE OF ART is the lifelong construction of a state of wonder.

Glenn Gould

❧ ❧ ❧ ❧

IF THE WORLD SHOULD blow itself up, the last audible voice would be that of an expert saying it can't be done.

Peter Ustinov

❧ ❧ ❧ ❧

THE DOG is the god of frolic.

Henry Ward Beecher

❧ ❧ ❧ ❧

EVERYTHING ON THE EARTH has a purpose, every disease an herb to cure it, and every person a mission. This is the Indian theory of existence.

Mourning Dove

❧ ❧ ❧ ❧

ALL EXPERIENCE is an arch, to build upon.

Henry Adams

❧ ❧ ❧ ❧

LOVE IS A SNOWMOBILE racing across the tundra and then suddenly it flips over, pinning you underneath. At night, the ice weasels come.

Matt Groening

❧ ❧ ❧ ❧

LIBERTY IS ALWAYS dangerous—but it is the safest thing we have.

Harry Emerson Fosdick

❧ ❧ ❧ ❧

THE BEST EDUCATED human being is the one who understands most about the life in which he is placed.

Helen Keller

✦ ✦ ✦ ✦

HE WHO WOULD teach men to die would teach them to live.

Michel de Montaigne

✦ ✦ ✦ ✦

WHEN ONE PERSON SUFFERS from a delusion it is called insanity. When many people suffer from a delusion it is called Religion.

Robert M. Pirsig

✦ ✦ ✦ ✦

YOU'RE ENOUGH TO TRY the patience of an oyster!

Lewis Carroll

✦ ✦ ✦ ✦

PEOPLE SEEM TO ENJOY things more when they know a lot of other people have been left out of the pleasure.

Russell Baker

✦ ✦ ✦ ✦

KNOW THE ENEMY and know yourself; in a hundred battles, you will never be in peril.

Sun Tzu

✦ ✦ ✦ ✦

REGRET FOR THE THINGS we did can be tempered by time; it is regret for the things we did not do that is inconsolable.

Sydney J. Harris

❧ ❧ ❧ ❧

WHAT IS RATIONAL is actual and what is actual is rational.

Georg Wilhelm Friedrich Hegel

❧ ❧ ❧ ❧

THE WORST SIN towards our fellow creatures is not to hate them, but to be indifferent to them; that's the essence of inhumanity.

George Bernard Shaw

❧ ❧ ❧ ❧

WE ARE JUST AN ADVANCED breed of monkeys on a minor planet of a very average star. But we can understand the Universe. That makes us something very special.

Stephen Hawking

❧ ❧ ❧ ❧

I FEEL BAD that I don't feel worse.

Michael Frayn

❧ ❧ ❧ ❧

THE GREATER LOVE is a mother's; then comes a dog's; then a sweetheart's.

Polish proverb

❧ ❧ ❧ ❧

MEMORY IS THE DIARY that we all carry about with us.

Oscar Wilde

❧ ❧ ❧ ❧

THE SECRET OF GENIUS is to carry the spirit of the child into old age, which means never losing your enthusiasm.

Victor Hugo

❧ ❧ ❧ ❧

THIS IS THE WAY the world ends: not with a bang but a whimper.

T. S. Eliot

❧ ❧ ❧ ❧

WE'RE OUR OWN dragons as well as our own heroes, and we have to rescue ourselves from ourselves.

Tom Robbins

❧ ❧ ❧ ❧

THOUGH A GOOD DEAL is too strange to be believed, nothing is too strange to have happened.

Thomas Hardy

❧ ❧ ❧ ❧

THEY ARE MUCH TO BE PITIED who have not been given a taste for nature early in life.

Jane Austen

❧ ❧ ❧ ❧

THE JURY SYSTEM puts a ban upon intelligence and honesty, and a premium upon ignorance, stupidity, and perjury.

Mark Twain

❧ ❧ ❧ ❧

THERE ARE ONLY TWO WAYS to live your life. One is as though nothing is a miracle. The other is as though everything is a miracle.

Albert Einstein

❧ ❧ ❧ ❧

ART IS THE OBJECTIFICATION of feeling, and the subjectification of nature.

Susanne K. Langer

❧ ❧ ❧ ❧

TRY TO LEARN SOMETHING about everything and everything about something.

Thomas Henry Huxley

❧ ❧ ❧ ❧

A TEACHER AFFECTS ETERNITY; he can never tell where his influence stops.

Henry Adams

❧ ❧ ❧ ❧

THE WORLD IS ALL GATES, all opportunities, strings of tension waiting to be struck.

Ralph Waldo Emerson

❧ ❧ ❧ ❧

THERE MUST BE QUITE a few things a hot bath won't cure, but I don't know many of them.

Sylvia Plath

❧ ❧ ❧ ❧

NOTHING IS PARTICULARLY hard if you divide it into small jobs.

Henry Ford

❧ ❧ ❧ ❧

PERHAPS I KNOW BEST why it is man alone who laughs; he alone suffers so deeply that he had to invent laughter.

Friedrich Nietzsche

❧ ❧ ❧ ❧

THE CRIMINAL IS THE CREATIVE ARTIST; the detective only the critic.

G. K. Chesterton

❧ ❧ ❧ ❧

IF THERE IS A WRONG THING to do, it will be done, infallibly. One has come to believe in that as if it were a law of nature.

George Orwell

❧ ❧ ❧ ❧

DEMOCRACY SUBSTITUTES election by the incompetent many for appointment by the corrupt few.

George Bernard Shaw

❧ ❧ ❧ ❧

EVERYBODY GETS SO MUCH information all day long that they lose their common sense.

Gertrude Stein

✿ ✿ ✿ ✿

THE PURPOSE of life is a life of purpose.

Robert Byrne

✿ ✿ ✿ ✿

NOTHING THAT IS WORTH knowing can be taught.

Oscar Wilde

✿ ✿ ✿ ✿

IT TAKES ALL THE RUNNING you can do, to keep in the same place.

Lewis Carroll

✿ ✿ ✿ ✿

HOLD FAST TO DREAMS
For if dreams die,
Life is like a broken-winged bird
That cannot fly.

Langston Hughes

✿ ✿ ✿ ✿

THE HUMAN BEING who would not harm you on an individual, face-to-face basis, who is charitable, civic-minded, loving and devout, will wound or kill you from behind the corporate veil.

Morton Mintz

✿ ✿ ✿ ✿

SEEK SIMPLICITY and distrust it.

Alfred North Whitehead

❧ ❧ ❧ ❧

GIVE ME A CHILD and I'll shape him into anything.

B. F. Skinner

❧ ❧ ❧ ❧

WOMAN DOES NOT FORGET that she needs the fecundator; she does not forget that everything that is born of her is planted in her.

Anaïs Nin

❧ ❧ ❧ ❧

I'VE DEVELOPED a new philosophy...I only dread one day at a time.

Charles Schulz

❧ ❧ ❧ ❧

PEOPLE OUGHT TO BE ONE of two things, young or old. No—what's the good of fooling? People ought to be one of two things, young or dead.

Dorothy Parker

❧ ❧ ❧ ❧

HE ATTACKED EVERYTHING in life with a mixture of extraordinary genius and naïve incompetence, and it was often difficult to tell which was which.

Douglas Adams

❧ ❧ ❧ ❧

FOLLOW YOUR INSTINCTS. That's where true wisdom manifests itself.

Oprah Winfrey

❖ ❖ ❖ ❖

I THINK THAT PEOPLE want peace so much that one of these days governments had better get out of the way and let them have it.

Dwight D. Eisenhower

❖ ❖ ❖ ❖

PEOPLE WILL NOT LOOK forward to posterity, who never look backward to their ancestors.

Edmund Burke

❖ ❖ ❖ ❖

WHAT A LOVELY SURPRISE to finally discover how unlonely being alone can be.

Ellen Burstyn

❖ ❖ ❖ ❖

THERE ARE NO SECOND acts in American lives.

F. Scott Fitzgerald

❖ ❖ ❖ ❖

A CONFERENCE IS A GATHERING of important people who singly can do nothing but together can decide that nothing can be done.

Fred Allen

❖ ❖ ❖ ❖

NO, I DON'T UNDERSTAND my husband's theory of relativity, but I know my husband and I know he can be trusted.

Elsa Einstein

❖ ❖ ❖ ❖

WICKEDNESS IS A MYTH invented by good people to account for the curious attractiveness of others.

Oscar Wilde

❖ ❖ ❖ ❖

IT IS AS NATURAL to die as to be born.

Francis Bacon

❖ ❖ ❖ ❖

IF YOUR LIFE IS BURNING WELL, poetry is just the ash.

Leonard Cohen

❖ ❖ ❖ ❖

I ALWAYS WANTED to be somebody, but I see now I should have been more specific.

Lily Tomlin

❖ ❖ ❖ ❖

THERE IS NO DEMOCRACY in physics. We can't say that some second-rate guy has as much right to opinion as Fermi.

Luis Walter Alvarez

❖ ❖ ❖ ❖

THERE IS NOTHING we receive with so much reluctance as advice.

Joseph Addison

⚜ ⚜ ⚜ ⚜

HISTORY IS THE SUM TOTAL of all the things that could have been avoided.

Konrad Adenauer

⚜ ⚜ ⚜ ⚜

THE QUALITY OF IDEAS seems to play a minor role in mass movement leadership. What counts is the arrogant gesture, the complete disregard of the opinion of others, the single-handed defiance of the world.

Eric Hoffer

⚜ ⚜ ⚜ ⚜

HE WHO CONQUERS others is strong. He who conquers himself is mighty.

Lao Tzu

⚜ ⚜ ⚜ ⚜

ONLY THROUGH ART can we get outside ourselves and know another's view of the universe.

Marcel Proust

⚜ ⚜ ⚜ ⚜

LOYALTY TO PETRIFIED opinions never yet broke a chain or freed a human soul in this world—and never will.

Mark Twain

⚜ ⚜ ⚜ ⚜

LIFE IS LIKE A DOGSLED TEAM. If you ain't the lead dog, the scenery never changes.

Lewis Grizzard

✣ ✣ ✣ ✣

I LIKE THE DREAMS of the future better than the history of the past.

Thomas Jefferson

✣ ✣ ✣ ✣

IF THERE WERE A VERB meaning "to believe falsely," it would not have any significant first person, present indicative.

Ludwig Wittgenstein

✣ ✣ ✣ ✣

DREAMS ARE ILLUSTRATIONS ... from the book your soul is writing about you.

Marsha Norman

✣ ✣ ✣ ✣

SOLITUDE IS THE PROFOUNDEST fact of the human condition. Man is the only being who knows he is alone, and the only one who seeks out another.

Octavio Paz

✣ ✣ ✣ ✣

WISE MEN TALK because they have something to say; fools, because they have to say something.

Plato

✣ ✣ ✣ ✣

SHOW ME A SANE man and I will cure him for you.

Carl Jung

❧ ❧ ❧ ❧

IF YOU DON'T LIVE the only life you have, you won't live some other life, you won't live any life at all.

James Baldwin

❧ ❧ ❧ ❧

EVERYBODY CAN BE GREAT, because everybody can serve.

Dr. Martin Luther King, Jr.

❧ ❧ ❧ ❧

IT IS BY FORGIVING that one is forgiven.

Mother Teresa

❧ ❧ ❧ ❧

WHO KNOWS BUT THAT, on the lower frequencies, I speak for you?

Ralph Ellison

❧ ❧ ❧ ❧

IT IS A PARADOXICAL but profoundly true and important principle of life that the most likely way to reach a goal is to be aiming not at that goal itself but at some more ambitious goal beyond it.

Arnold J. Toynbee

❧ ❧ ❧ ❧

TACT IS THE ABILITY to describe others as they see themselves.

Abraham Lincoln

⚜ ⚜ ⚜ ⚜

IT IS ALMOST IMPOSSIBLE systematically to constitute a natural moral law. Nature has no principles. She furnishes us with no reason to believe that human life is to be respected. Nature, in her indifference, makes no distinction between good and evil.

Anatole France

⚜ ⚜ ⚜ ⚜

DAYS AND MONTHS are travelers of eternity. So are the years that pass by.

Matsuo Basho

⚜ ⚜ ⚜ ⚜

COURAGE IS THE FEAR of being thought a coward.

Horace Smith

⚜ ⚜ ⚜ ⚜

THE HAND THAT HOLDS the quill controls history.

Charles L. Blockson

⚜ ⚜ ⚜ ⚜

ONE ORIGINAL THOUGHT is worth a thousand mindless quotings.

Diogenes

⚜ ⚜ ⚜ ⚜

THE UNCONSCIOUS is structured like a language.

Jacques Lacan

❖ ❖ ❖ ❖

THERE ARE SOME LAUGHS you have in life, provided by comedians and provided by fortuitous moments with your family or friends or something. But most of it is tragic. You're born, you don't know why. You're here, you don't know why. You go, you die. Your family dies. Your friends die. People suffer. People live in constant terror. The world is full of poverty and corruption and war and Nazis and tsunamis. . . . The net result, the final count is, you lose; you don't beat the house.

Woody Allen

❖ ❖ ❖ ❖

FACTS are the enemy of truth.

Miguel de Cervantes

❖ ❖ ❖ ❖

DREAMS ARE TODAY'S answers to tomorrow's questions.

Edgar Cayce

❖ ❖ ❖ ❖

NOTHING WHICH IS AT ALL TIMES and in every way agreeable to us can have objective reality. It is of the very nature of the real that it should have sharp corners and rough edges, that it should be resistant, should be itself. Dream-furniture is the only kind on which you never stub your toes or bang your knee.

C. S. Lewis

❖ ❖ ❖ ❖

TO SEE WHAT IS IN FRONT of one's nose needs a constant struggle.

George Orwell

✤ ✤ ✤ ✤

WITHOUT THE POSSIBILITY of suicide, I would have killed myself long ago.

E. M. Cioran

✤ ✤ ✤ ✤

GOSSIP IS THE OPIATE of the oppressed.

Erica Jong

✤ ✤ ✤ ✤

WRITING IS SO DIFFICULT that I often feel that writers, having had their hell on earth, will escape all punishment hereafter.

Jessamyn West

✤ ✤ ✤ ✤

A THING OF BEAUTY is a joy for ever;
Its loveliness increases; it will never
Pass into nothingness; but still will keep
A bower quiet for us, and a sleep
Full of sweet dreams, and health, and quiet breathing.

John Keats

✤ ✤ ✤ ✤

WE ARE NOT HYPOCRITES in our sleep.

William Hazlitt

✤ ✤ ✤ ✤

AFTER SILENCE, that which comes nearest to expressing the inexpressible is music.

Aldous Huxley

⚜ ⚜ ⚜ ⚜

IN THE UNITED STATES there is more space where nobody is than where anybody is. That is what makes America what it is.

Gertrude Stein

⚜ ⚜ ⚜ ⚜

THE GREATEST THING in the world is to know how to belong to oneself.

Michel de Montaigne

⚜ ⚜ ⚜ ⚜

ONLY MEDIOCRITY can be trusted to be always at its best.

Max Beerbohm

⚜ ⚜ ⚜ ⚜

ALL NEWSPAPER and journalistic activity is an intellectual brothel from which there is no retreat.

Leo Tolstoy

⚜ ⚜ ⚜ ⚜

TELEVISION . . . IS A MEDIUM of entertainment which permits millions of people to listen to the same joke at the same time, and yet remain lonesome.

T. S. Eliot

⚜ ⚜ ⚜ ⚜

THE PAST IS OUR DEFINITION. We may strive, with good reason, to escape it, or to escape what is bad in it, but we will escape it only by adding something better to it.

Wendell Berry

❖ ❖ ❖ ❖

THE ETERNAL MYSTERY of the world is its comprehensibility.... The fact that it is comprehensible is a miracle.

Albert Einstein

❖ ❖ ❖ ❖

THE ULTIMATE TEST of a moral society is the kind of world that it leaves to its children.

Dietrich Bonhoeffer

❖ ❖ ❖ ❖

NOTHING IN LIFE is to be feared. It is only to be understood.

Marie Curie

❖ ❖ ❖ ❖

MEN BEING ... BY NATURE all free, equal, and independent, no one can be put out of this estate, and subjected to the political power of another, without his own consent.

John Locke

❖ ❖ ❖ ❖

BOOKS ARE GOOD enough in their own way, but they are a mighty bloodless substitute for life.

Robert Louis Stevenson

❖ ❖ ❖ ❖

SOMETIMES IT SEEMS the only accomplishment my education ever bestowed on me was the ability to think in quotations.

Margaret Drabble

❖ ❖ ❖ ❖

LIFE IS A GAMBLE at terrible odds. If it was a bet, you would not take it.

Tom Stoppard

❖ ❖ ❖ ❖

THE HARDEST THING to learn in life is which bridge to cross and which to burn.

Laurence J. Peter

❖ ❖ ❖ ❖

IF YOU CAN WALK you can dance. If you can talk you can sing.

Zimbabwean proverb

❖ ❖ ❖ ❖

POETRY IS A DEAL of joy and pain and wonder, with a dash of the dictionary.

Kahlil Gibran

❖ ❖ ❖ ❖

IT IS IMPOSSIBLE for me to envisage a picture as being other than a window, and . . . my first concern is then to know what it looks out on.

André Breton

❖ ❖ ❖ ❖

IMAGINATION WILL OFTEN carry us to worlds that never were. But without it we go nowhere.

Carl Sagan

❧ ❧ ❧ ❧

THE ONLY THING that can save the world is the reclaiming of the awareness of the world. That's what poetry does.

Allen Ginsberg

❧ ❧ ❧ ❧

WHEN WE CLAIM to "remember" our pasts, we are surely remembering our favorite snapshots, in which the long-faded past is given a distinct visual immortality.

Joyce Carol Oates

❧ ❧ ❧ ❧

I WAS IN LOVE with the whole world and all that lived in its rainy arms.

Louise Erdrich

❧ ❧ ❧ ❧

A SCHOLAR WHO CHERISHES the love of comfort is not fit to be deemed a scholar.

Lao Tzu

❧ ❧ ❧ ❧

GENIUS IS ANOTHER WORD for magic, and the whole point of magic is that it is inexplicable.

Margot Fonteyn

❧ ❧ ❧ ❧

BEGIN AT THE BEGINNING and go on till you come to the end; then stop.

Lewis Carroll

⚜ ⚜ ⚜ ⚜

SOME MEN ARE BORN MEDIOCRE, some men achieve mediocrity, and some men have mediocrity thrust upon them.

Joseph Heller

⚜ ⚜ ⚜ ⚜

THERE AIN'T NO MAN CAN avoid being born average. But there ain't no man got to be common.

Satchel Paige

⚜ ⚜ ⚜ ⚜

IN CHARITY there is no excess.

Francis Bacon

⚜ ⚜ ⚜ ⚜

SUCCESS IS THE ABILITY to go from one failure to another with no loss of enthusiasm.

Winston Churchill

⚜ ⚜ ⚜ ⚜

EVERY GREAT MISTAKE has a halfway moment, a split second when it can be recalled and perhaps remedied.

Pearl Buck

⚜ ⚜ ⚜ ⚜

EXPERIENCE WAS of no ethical value. It was merely the name men gave to their mistakes.

Oscar Wilde

✣ ✣ ✣ ✣

[ON DRAWING:] AN ACTIVE LINE on a walk, moving freely without a goal. A walk for a walk's sake.

Paul Klee

✣ ✣ ✣ ✣

THERE MAY BE SAID to be two classes of people in the world: those who constantly divide the people of the world into two classes, and those who do not.

Robert Benchley

✣ ✣ ✣ ✣

LIFE ISN'T A MATTER of milestones, but of moments.

Rose Fitzgerald Kennedy

✣ ✣ ✣ ✣

WE'RE ALL OF US SENTENCED to solitary confinement inside our own skins, for life!

Tennessee Williams

✣ ✣ ✣ ✣

YOU'VE ACHIEVED SUCCESS in your field when you don't know whether what you're doing is work or play.

Warren Beatty

✣ ✣ ✣ ✣

THE FUTURE INFLUENCES the present just as much as the past.

Friedrich Nietzsche

⚜ ⚜ ⚜ ⚜

ALTHOUGH HUMAN LIFE is priceless, we always act as if something had an even greater price than life. But what is that something?

Antoine de Saint-Exupéry

⚜ ⚜ ⚜ ⚜

A THICK SKIN is a gift from God.

Konrad Adenauer

⚜ ⚜ ⚜ ⚜

I DON'T DESERVE THIS AWARD, but I have arthritis and I don't deserve that either.

Jack Benny

⚜ ⚜ ⚜ ⚜

A POEM BEGINS AS A LUMP in the throat, a sense of wrong, a homesickness, a lovesickness.

Robert Frost

⚜ ⚜ ⚜ ⚜

THERE CAN'T BE ANY large-scale revolution until there's a personal revolution, on an individual level. It's got to happen inside first.

Jim Morrison

⚜ ⚜ ⚜ ⚜

DULLNESS is a misdemeanor.

Ethel Wilson

❧ ❧ ❧ ❧

WE OFTEN GIVE OUR ENEMIES the means for our own destruction.

Aesop

❧ ❧ ❧ ❧

A MAN HAS NO BUSINESS to be depressed by a disappointment, anyway; he ought to make up his mind to get even.

Mark Twain

❧ ❧ ❧ ❧

THE TEACHER WHO . . . is indeed wise does not bid you to enter the house of his wisdom, but rather leads you to the threshold of your own mind.

Kahlil Gibran

❧ ❧ ❧ ❧

WE MAY NOT RETURN the affection of those who like us, but we always respect their good judgment.

Libbie Fudim

❧ ❧ ❧ ❧

ETERNITY IS A TERRIBLE thought. I mean, where's it going to end?

Tom Stoppard

❧ ❧ ❧ ❧

WHEN YOU DON'T HAVE any money, the problem is food. When you have money, it's sex. When you have both, it's health. If everything is simply jake, then you're frightened of death.

J. P. Donleavy

❧ ❧ ❧ ❧

YOU CAN TELL THE SIZE of a man by the size of the thing that makes him mad.

Adlai Stevenson

❧ ❧ ❧ ❧

IF MEN WERE EQUAL tomorrow and all wore the same coats, they would wear different coats the next day.

Anthony Trollope

❧ ❧ ❧ ❧

IF THIS IS DYING, then I don't think much of it.

Lytton Strachey

❧ ❧ ❧ ❧

IN A BUREAUCRATIC SYSTEM, useless work drives out useful work.

Milton Friedman

❧ ❧ ❧ ❧

WE ALL KNOW THAT ART is not truth. Art is a lie that makes us realize truth.

Pablo Picasso

❧ ❧ ❧ ❧

HALF OUR LIFE IS SPENT trying to find something to do with the time we have rushed through life trying to save.

Will Rogers

❖ ❖ ❖ ❖

ONLY THE TINIEST fraction of mankind want freedom. All the rest want someone to tell them they are free.

Irving Layton

❖ ❖ ❖ ❖

TO BE ADULT is to be alone.

Jean Rostand

❖ ❖ ❖ ❖

FOR HATE IS NOT CONQUERED by hate: Hate is conquered by love. This is a law eternal.

Pali Tripitaka

❖ ❖ ❖ ❖

I NEVER WANTED to be famous. I only wanted to be great.

Ray Charles

❖ ❖ ❖ ❖

A MAN SAID TO THE UNIVERSE: "Sir, I exist!" "However," replied the universe, "The fact has not created in me a sense of obligation."

Stephen Crane

❖ ❖ ❖ ❖

LIFE IS WHAT HAPPENS to us while we are busy making other plans.

Allen Saunders

✠ ✠ ✠ ✠

ALL ARE LUNATICS, but he who can analyze his delusions is called a philosopher.

Ambrose Bierce

✠ ✠ ✠ ✠

WHEN A MAN POINTS a finger at someone else, he should remember that four of his fingers are pointing to himself.

Louis Nizer

✠ ✠ ✠ ✠

WE ARE NOT HUMAN BEINGS on a spiritual journey. We are spiritual beings on a human journey.

Steven Covey

✠ ✠ ✠ ✠

IN SCIENCE, "FACT" can only mean "confirmed to such a degree that it would be perverse to withhold provisional assent."

Stephen Jay Gould

✠ ✠ ✠ ✠

HEROES ARE PEOPLE who rise to the occasion and slip quietly away.

Tom Brokaw

✠ ✠ ✠ ✠

COMMUNISM is like one big phone company.

Lenny Bruce

✣ ✣ ✣ ✣

ANY SYSTEM OF RELIGION that has any thing in it that shocks the mind of a child cannot be a true system.

Thomas Paine

✣ ✣ ✣ ✣

NO AMOUNT OF EXPERIMENTATION can ever prove me right; a single experiment can prove me wrong.

Albert Einstein

✣ ✣ ✣ ✣

FOR A MAN TO ACHIEVE all that is demanded of him he must regard himself as greater than he is.

Johann Wolfgang von Goethe

✣ ✣ ✣ ✣

HAPPINESS LIES in the consciousness we have of it.

George Sand

✣ ✣ ✣ ✣

THERE IS ONLY ONE THING about which I am certain, and that is that there is very little about which one can be certain.

W. Somerset Maugham

✣ ✣ ✣ ✣

I SHALL NOT DIE OF A COLD. I shall die of having lived.

Willa Cather

✤ ✤ ✤ ✤

GREAT MEN can't be ruled.

Ayn Rand

✤ ✤ ✤ ✤

I REMEMBER MY YOUTH and the feeling that will never come back any more—the feeling that I could last for ever, outlast the sea, the earth, and all men; the deceitful feeling that lures us on to joys, to perils, to love, to vain effort—to death; the triumphant conviction of strength, the heat of life in the handful of dust, the glow in the heart that with every year grows dim, grows cold, grows small, and expires—and expires, too soon, too soon—before life itself.

Joseph Conrad

✤ ✤ ✤ ✤

WE ARE ALL BORN MAD. Some remain so.

Samuel Beckett

✤ ✤ ✤ ✤

FRIENDS MAY COME AND GO, but enemies accumulate.

Thomas Jones

✤ ✤ ✤ ✤

TO TEACH is to learn twice.

Joseph Joubert

✤ ✤ ✤ ✤

WHINING is anger through a small opening.

Al Franken

❧ ❧ ❧ ❧

I'M A SLOW WALKER, but I never walk back.

Abraham Lincoln

❧ ❧ ❧ ❧

LIFE IS FULL OF MISERY, loneliness, and suffering—and it's all over much too soon.

Woody Allen

❧ ❧ ❧ ❧

IF THE DREAMS of any so-called normal man were exposed... there would be no more gravity and dignity left for mankind.

Vera Caspary

❧ ❧ ❧ ❧

WHOEVER DESTROYS a single life is as guilty as though he had destroyed the entire world; and whoever rescues a single life earns as much merit as though he had rescued the entire world.

Talmud

❧ ❧ ❧ ❧

ANYTHING THAT YOU are good at contributes to happiness.

Bertrand Russell

❧ ❧ ❧ ❧

I MAY HAVE FAULTS but being wrong ain't one of them.

Jimmy Hoffa

❧ ❧ ❧ ❧

BEFORE ENLIGHTENMENT—chop wood, carry water. After enlightenment—chop wood, carry water.

Zen proverb

❧ ❧ ❧ ❧

I HAVE FOUND LITTLE that is "good" about human beings on the whole. In my experience, most of them are trash.

Sigmund Freud

❧ ❧ ❧ ❧

DON'T BELIEVE THE WORLD owes you a living; the world owes you nothing—it was here first.

Robert Jones Burdette

❧ ❧ ❧ ❧

A CYNIC IS NOT MERELY one who reads bitter lessons from the past; he is one who is prematurely disappointed in the future.

Sydney J. Harris

❧ ❧ ❧ ❧

IT IS SUCH A SECRET PLACE, the land of tears.

Antoine de Saint-Exupéry

❧ ❧ ❧ ❧

INTEGRITY has no need of rules.

Albert Camus

❧ ❧ ❧ ❧

LIKE ALL WEAK MEN he laid an exaggerated stress on not changing one's mind.

W. Somerset Maugham

❧ ❧ ❧ ❧

WE HAVE WATERED the trees that blossom in the summer-time. Now let's sprinkle those whose flowering-time is past. That will be a better deed because we shall not be working for a reward.

Kalidasa

❧ ❧ ❧ ❧

MAN, WHEN PERFECTED, is the best of animals, but, when separated from law and justice, he is the worst of all.

Aristotle

❧ ❧ ❧ ❧

KNOW thyself.

Anonymous

❧ ❧ ❧ ❧

A MAN IS A SUCCESS if he gets up in the morning and goes to bed at night and in between does what he wants to do.

Bob Dylan

❧ ❧ ❧ ❧

THE BASIC CONCEPT of the Dilbert Principle is that the most ineffective workers are systematically moved to the place where they can do the least damage: management.

Scott Adams

✤ ✤ ✤ ✤

COURAGE IS FEAR holding on a minute longer.

George S. Patton

✤ ✤ ✤ ✤

READING MAKES IMMIGRANTS of us all. It takes us away from home, but more important, it finds homes for us everywhere.

Jean Rhys

✤ ✤ ✤ ✤

RESEARCH IS THE PROCESS of going up alleys to see if they are blind.

Marston Bates

✤ ✤ ✤ ✤

SOMETIMES THE ROAD less traveled is less traveled for a reason.

Jerry Seinfeld

✤ ✤ ✤ ✤

SUCCESS IS PEACE OF MIND which is a direct result of self-satisfaction in knowing you made the effort to do the best of which you are capable.

John Wooden

✤ ✤ ✤ ✤

MIRACLES ARE PROPITIOUS ACCIDENTS, the natural causes of which are too complicated to be readily understood.

George Santayana

❧ ❧ ❧ ❧

ALL THAT MANKIND has done, thought, gained or been: it is lying as in magic preservation in the pages of books.

Thomas Carlyle

❧ ❧ ❧ ❧

THE READING OF ALL GOOD BOOKS is like a conversation with the most eminent people of past centuries.

René Descartes

❧ ❧ ❧ ❧

SOMETIMES I WONDER if men and women really suit each other. Perhaps they should live next door and just visit now and then.

Katharine Hepburn

❧ ❧ ❧ ❧

LANGUAGE IS A FORM of organized stutter.

Marshall McLuhan

❧ ❧ ❧ ❧

SO IT GOES.

Kurt Vonnegut

❧ ❧ ❧ ❧

TO BE WILLING to die for an idea is to set a rather high price on conjecture.

Anatole France

❧ ❧ ❧ ❧

CONSCIENCE DOES MAKE cowards of us all.

William Shakespeare

❧ ❧ ❧ ❧

CRIME, like virtue, has its degrees.

Jean Racine

❧ ❧ ❧ ❧

ALL MY LIFE I have lived and behaved very much like the sandpiper—just running down the edges of different countries and continents looking for something.

Elizabeth Bishop

❧ ❧ ❧ ❧

A GOAL WITHOUT a plan is just a wish.

Antoine de Saint-Exupéry

❧ ❧ ❧ ❧

THERE ARE TWO DILEMMAS that rattle the human skull: How do you hang on to someone who won't stay? And how do you get rid of someone who won't go?

Danny DeVito

❧ ❧ ❧ ❧

I AM A GREAT BELIEVER in luck, and I find that the harder I work the more luck I have.

Thomas Jefferson

❧ ❧ ❧ ❧

A DIRECTOR MAKES only one film in his life. Then he breaks it into pieces and makes it again.

Jean Renoir

❧ ❧ ❧ ❧

THERE CAN BE NO REAL FREEDOM without the freedom to fail.

Eric Hoffer

❧ ❧ ❧ ❧

NEVER LOOK DOWN to test the ground before taking your next step; only he who keeps his eye fixed on the far horizon will find his right road.

Dag Hammarskjöld

❧ ❧ ❧ ❧

WE NEED A REVOLUTION inside of our own minds.

John Henrik Clarke

❧ ❧ ❧ ❧

WITHOUT LEAPS of imagination, or dreaming, we lose the excitement of possibilities. Dreaming, after all, is a form of planning.

Gloria Steinem

❧ ❧ ❧ ❧

I'M IN FAVOR OF FREE EXPRESSION provided it's kept rigidly under control.

Alan Bennett

❧ ❧ ❧ ❧

GOOD IS NOT GOOD, where better is expected.

Thomas Fuller

❧ ❧ ❧ ❧

THANK GOD, men cannot as yet fly, and lay waste the sky as well as the earth.

Henry David Thoreau

❧ ❧ ❧ ❧

WORSE, TO HAVE LIVED without even attempting to lay claim to one's portion of the earth; to have lived and died as one has been born, unnecessary and unaccommodated.

V. S. Naipaul

❧ ❧ ❧ ❧

THE SUREST SIGN that intelligent life exists elsewhere in the universe is that none of it has ever tried to contact us.

Bill Watterson

❧ ❧ ❧ ❧

ONE OF THE MOST striking differences between a cat and a lie is that a cat has only nine lives.

Mark Twain

❧ ❧ ❧ ❧

THERE IS ONLY ONE THING in the world worse than being talked about, and that is not being talked about.

Oscar Wilde

❧ ❧ ❧ ❧

AMERICA, I've given you all and now I'm nothing.

Allen Ginsberg

❧ ❧ ❧ ❧

THE EMPIRES OF THE FUTURE are the empires of the mind.

Winston Churchill

❧ ❧ ❧ ❧

THE MEMORIES will be so thick that the outfielders will have to brush them away from their faces.

W. P. Kinsella

❧ ❧ ❧ ❧

TO LIVE ONLY for some future goal is shallow. It's the sides of the mountain that sustain life, not the top.

Robert M. Pirsig

❧ ❧ ❧ ❧

INTELLECTUALS ARE PEOPLE who believe that ideas are of more importance than values; that is to say, their own ideas and other people's values.

Gerald Brenan

❧ ❧ ❧ ❧

FORGET ABOUT LIKES and dislikes. They are of no consequence. Just do what must be done. This may not be happiness, but it is greatness.

George Bernard Shaw

�֍ ✦ ✦ ✦

ACCENTUATE THE POSITIVES; medicate the negatives.

Amy Sedaris

✦ ✦ ✦ ✦

GREATER THINGS are believed of those who are absent.

Tacitus

✦ ✦ ✦ ✦

WE ARE SPINNING our own fates, good or evil, never to be undone.

William James

✦ ✦ ✦ ✦

LIFE IS A SERIES of collisions with the future; it is not the sum of what we have been but what we yearn to be.

José Ortega y Gasset

✦ ✦ ✦ ✦

CALLING WOMEN the weaker sex makes about as much sense as calling men the stronger one.

Gladiola Montana

✦ ✦ ✦ ✦

AN INSTITUTION is the lengthening shadow of one man.

Ralph Waldo Emerson

❧ ❧ ❧ ❧

NOTHING TRAVELS FASTER than the speed of light with the possible exception of bad news, which obeys its own special laws.

Douglas Adams

❧ ❧ ❧ ❧

MOCKINGBIRDS DON'T DO one thing but make music for us to enjoy… [they] sing their hearts out for us. That's why it's a sin to kill a mockingbird.

Harper Lee

❧ ❧ ❧ ❧

THERE'S NOTHING THAT MAKES you so aware of the improvisation of human experience as a song unfinished. Or an old address book.

Carson McCullers

❧ ❧ ❧ ❧

EVERY TRUE PASSION thinks only of itself.

Stendhal

❧ ❧ ❧ ❧

THE AIM OF THE LIAR is simply to charm, to delight, to give pleasure. He is the very basis of civilized society.

Oscar Wilde

❧ ❧ ❧ ❧

IF A IS SUCCESS IN LIFE, then A equals x plus y plus z. Work is x; y is play; and z is keeping your mouth shut.

Albert Einstein

⚜ ⚜ ⚜ ⚜

IT IS VERY EASY to forgive others their mistakes; it takes more grit and gumption to forgive them for having witnessed our own.

Jessamyn West

⚜ ⚜ ⚜ ⚜

SOME PEOPLE APPROACH every problem with an open mouth.

Adlai Stevenson

⚜ ⚜ ⚜ ⚜

LAZINESS IS NOTHING more than the habit of resting before you get tired.

Jules Renard

⚜ ⚜ ⚜ ⚜

WHAT WE CALL "PROGRESS" is the exchange of one nuisance for another nuisance.

Havelock Ellis

⚜ ⚜ ⚜ ⚜

A PROUD MAN IS SELDOM a grateful man, for he never thinks he gets as much as he deserves.

Henry Ward Beecher

⚜ ⚜ ⚜ ⚜

A GOOD INDIGNATION brings out all one's powers.

Ralph Waldo Emerson

❧ ❧ ❧ ❧

EVERY FORM OF ADDICTION is bad, no matter whether the narcotic be alcohol or morphine or idealism.

Carl Jung

❧ ❧ ❧ ❧

MAN WAS BORN FREE and everywhere he is in shackles.

Jean-Jacques Rousseau

❧ ❧ ❧ ❧

HOW WOULD YOU like to stand like a god before the crest of a monster billow, always rushing to the bottom of a hill and never reaching its base, and to come rushing in for a half mile at express speed, in graceful attitude, of course, until you reach the beach and step easily from the wave to the strand?

Duke Kahanamoku

❧ ❧ ❧ ❧

NOSTALGIA is a seductive liar.

George W. Ball

❧ ❧ ❧ ❧

NO VICTOR believes in chance.

Friedrich Nietzsche

❧ ❧ ❧ ❧

A RECESSION IS WHEN a neighbor loses his job. A depression is when you lose yours.

Anonymous

❖ ❖ ❖ ❖

IN POLITICS, nothing happens by accident. If it happens, you can bet it was planned that way.

Franklin Delano Roosevelt

❖ ❖ ❖ ❖

YOU ONLY HAVE to do a very few things right in your life so long as you don't do too many things wrong.

Warren Buffett

❖ ❖ ❖ ❖

TRUE EXCELLENCE is rarely found, even more, rarely is it cherished.

Johann Wolfgang von Goethe

❖ ❖ ❖ ❖

THERE ARE NOT ENOUGH JAILS, not enough policemen, not enough courts to enforce a law not supported by the people.

Hubert H. Humphrey

❖ ❖ ❖ ❖

CRIME IS A SOCIOPOLITICAL artifact, not a natural phenomenon. We can have as much or as little crime as we please, depending on what we choose to count as criminal.

Herbert L. Packer

❖ ❖ ❖ ❖

IF YOU WOULD not be forgotten, as soon as you are dead and rotten, either write things worth reading, or do things worth the writing.

Benjamin Franklin

✤ ✤ ✤ ✤

IF THE YOUNG ONLY KNEW; if the old only could.

French proverb

✤ ✤ ✤ ✤

I LOVE MYSELF when I am laughing.

Zora Neale Hurston

✤ ✤ ✤ ✤

I COULD DANCE with you till the cows come home. On second thought, I'd rather dance with the cows till you come home.

Groucho Marx

✤ ✤ ✤ ✤

IT IS BETTER TO DIE on your feet than to live on your knees!

Dolores Ibarruri

✤ ✤ ✤ ✤

CARPE DIEM! Rejoice while you are alive; Enjoy the day; live life to the fullest; Make the most of what you have. It is later than you think.

Horace

✤ ✤ ✤ ✤

HER BODY MOVED with the frankness that comes from solitary habits. But solitude is only a human presumption. Every quiet step is thunder to beetle life underfoot; every choice is a world made new for the chosen. All secrets are witnessed.

Barbara Kingsolver

❖ ❖ ❖ ❖

WHEN YOU LOOK into an abyss, the abyss also looks into you.

Friedrich Nietzsche

❖ ❖ ❖ ❖

SCIENCE HAS MADE us gods before we are even worthy of being men.

Jean Rostand

❖ ❖ ❖ ❖

ONE HALF OF THE WORLD cannot understand the pleasures of the other.

Jane Austen

❖ ❖ ❖ ❖

THE INTERPRETATION of dreams is the royal road to a knowledge of the unconscious activities of the mind.

Sigmund Freud

❖ ❖ ❖ ❖

I DON'T USE DRUGS, my dreams are frightening enough.

M. C. Escher

❖ ❖ ❖ ❖

I NEVER FORGIVE, but I always forget.

Arthur James Balfour

❖ ❖ ❖ ❖

WE ARE ALL IN THE GUTTER, but some of us are looking at the stars.

Oscar Wilde

❖ ❖ ❖ ❖

I PREFER THE WICKED rather than the foolish. The wicked sometimes rest.

Alexandre Dumas

❖ ❖ ❖ ❖

THE GREAT SPIRIT is in all things; he is in the air we breathe. The Great Spirit is our father, but the Earth is our mother. She nourishes us; that which we put into the ground she returns to us.

Big Thunder

❖ ❖ ❖ ❖

HOLLYWOOD'S A PLACE where they'll pay you a thousand dollars for a kiss, and fifty cents for your soul.

Marilyn Monroe

❖ ❖ ❖ ❖

IF I'M FREE, it's because I'm always running.

Jimi Hendrix

❖ ❖ ❖ ❖

IT WERE NOT BEST that we should all think alike; it is difference of opinion that makes horse races.

Mark Twain

❧ ❧ ❧ ❧

MIDDLE-CLASS ORDER is only disorder. Disorder to the point of paroxysm, deprived of all contact with the world of necessity.

René Magritte

❧ ❧ ❧ ❧

I CANNOT LIVE without books.

Thomas Jefferson

❧ ❧ ❧ ❧

THE BAD END UNHAPPILY, the good unluckily. That is what tragedy means.

Tom Stoppard

❧ ❧ ❧ ❧

SUCCESS IS ALWAYS more permanent when you achieve it without destroying your principles.

Walter Cronkite

❧ ❧ ❧ ❧

I WOULD LIKE to be the air
that inhabits you for a moment
only. I would like to be that unnoticed
& that necessary.

Margaret Atwood

❧ ❧ ❧ ❧

IF A THING IS WORTH DOING, it is worth doing badly.

G. K. Chesterton

❧ ❧ ❧ ❧

WE DON'T RECEIVE WISDOM; we must discover it for ourselves after a journey that no one can take for us or spare us.

Marcel Proust

❧ ❧ ❧ ❧

ALL HAPPY FAMILIES resemble one another, but each unhappy family is unhappy in its own way.

Leo Tolstoy

❧ ❧ ❧ ❧

EARTH IS A GREAT funhouse without the fun.

Jeff Berner

❧ ❧ ❧ ❧

WHEN I WAS 40, my doctor advised me that a man in his forties shouldn't play tennis. I heeded his advice carefully and could hardly wait until I reached 50 to start again.

Hugo L. Black

❧ ❧ ❧ ❧

SCIENCE is organized knowledge.

Herbert Spencer

❧ ❧ ❧ ❧

THE AVERAGE PH.D. thesis is nothing but the transference of bones from one graveyard to another.

J. Frank Dobie

❧ ❧ ❧ ❧

WHAT COSTS NOTHING is worth nothing.

Anonymous

❧ ❧ ❧ ❧

DESTINY IS AN INVENTION of the weak and the resigned.

Ignazio Silone

❧ ❧ ❧ ❧

IF YOU HATE A PERSON, you hate something in him that is part of yourself. What isn't part of ourselves doesn't disturb us.

Hermann Hesse

❧ ❧ ❧ ❧

WISDOM CONSISTS in being able to distinguish among dangers and make a choice of the least harmful.

Niccolò Machiavelli

❧ ❧ ❧ ❧

THERE ARE TIMES not to flirt. When you're sick. When you're with children. When you're on the witness stand.

Joyce Jillson

❧ ❧ ❧ ❧

THIS NATION CANNOT afford to be materially rich and spiritually poor.

John F. Kennedy

❖ ❖ ❖ ❖

LET YOUR HEAD be more than a funnel to your stomach.

Anonymous

❖ ❖ ❖ ❖

A LOT OF PEOPLE are afraid to say what they want. That's why they don't get what they want.

Madonna

❖ ❖ ❖ ❖

I HAVE LEARNED from experience that the greater part of our happiness or misery depends on our dispositions and not on our circumstances.

Martha Washington

❖ ❖ ❖ ❖

EDUCATION IS NOT the filling of a pail but the lighting of a fire

William Butler Yeats

❖ ❖ ❖ ❖

RISE EARLY AND THINK upon your deeds, and of the world to come; for you may be certain that the fruits of all your deeds will think upon you.

Sanskrit verse

❖ ❖ ❖ ❖

TAKE OUR POLITICIANS: they're a bunch of yo-yos. The presidency is now a cross between a popularity contest and a high school debate, with an encyclopedia of clichés the first prize.

Saul Bellow

❧ ❧ ❧ ❧

DYING IS AN ART, like everything else.

Sylvia Plath

❧ ❧ ❧ ❧

WITHOUT ART, the crudeness of reality would make the world unbearable.

George Bernard Shaw

❧ ❧ ❧ ❧

A MAN SHOULD LIVE if only to satisfy his curiosity.

Yiddish proverb

❧ ❧ ❧ ❧

ORIGINALITY, I FEAR, is too often only undetected and frequently unconscious plagiarism.

William Ralph Inge

❧ ❧ ❧ ❧

I WAS NOT LOOKING for my dreams to interpret my life, but rather for my life to interpret my dreams.

Susan Sontag

❧ ❧ ❧ ❧

THE OBSERVER, when he seems to himself to be observing a stone, is really, if physics is to be believed, observing the effects of the stone upon himself.

Bertrand Russell

⚜ ⚜ ⚜ ⚜

THERE IS BUT ONE ART, to omit.

Robert Louis Stevenson

⚜ ⚜ ⚜ ⚜

THE GREATEST PART of a writer's time is spent in reading, in order to write: A man will turn over half a library to make one book.

Samuel Johnson

⚜ ⚜ ⚜ ⚜

THE JOURNEY, not the arrival, matters.

Michel de Montaigne

⚜ ⚜ ⚜ ⚜

IF WE ARE TO KEEP our democracy, there must be one commandment: Thou shalt not ration justice.

Learned Hand

⚜ ⚜ ⚜ ⚜

TRUE TERROR is to wake up one morning and discover that your high school class is running the country.

Kurt Vonnegut

⚜ ⚜ ⚜ ⚜

WE GROW GREAT BY DREAMS. All big men are dreamers. They see things in the soft haze of a spring day or in the red fire of a long winter's evening. Some of us let these great dreams die, but others nourish and protect them, nurse them through bad days till they bring them to the sunshine and the light, which come always to those who sincerely hope that their dreams will come true.

Woodrow Wilson

⚜ ⚜ ⚜ ⚜

THE OBSTACLE is the path.

Zen proverb

⚜ ⚜ ⚜ ⚜

THE ONLY SURE THING about luck is that it will change.

Wilson Mizner

⚜ ⚜ ⚜ ⚜

WE KNOW WHAT WE ARE, but know not what we may be.

William Shakespeare

⚜ ⚜ ⚜ ⚜

IF THIS IS THE BEST of all possible worlds, what are the others like?

Voltaire

⚜ ⚜ ⚜ ⚜

A STUMBLE may prevent a fall.

English proverb

⚜ ⚜ ⚜ ⚜

WE KNOW WHAT happens to people who stay in the middle of the road. They get run over.

Aneurin Bevan

❖ ❖ ❖ ❖

80% OF SUCCESS is showing up.

Woody Allen

❖ ❖ ❖ ❖

FAMOUS REMARKS are very seldom quoted correctly.

Simeon Strunsky

❖ ❖ ❖ ❖

THE GREATEST DANGER for most of us is not that our aim is too high and we miss it, but that it is too low and we reach it.

Michelangelo

❖ ❖ ❖ ❖

YOU CAN'T MAKE UP anything anymore. The world itself is a satire. All you're doing is recording it.

Art Buchwald

❖ ❖ ❖ ❖

I HAVE FOUND that among its other benefits, giving liberates the soul of the giver.

Maya Angelou

❖ ❖ ❖ ❖

YOU ARE REMEMBERED for the rules you break.

Douglas MacArthur

✤ ✤ ✤ ✤

THE BASIS OF ART is truth, both in matter and in mode.

Flannery O'Connor

✤ ✤ ✤ ✤

THERE IS NO PLEASURE in having nothing to do; the fun is having lots to do and not doing it.

Andrew Jackson

✤ ✤ ✤ ✤

THE MOST EXHAUSTING thing in life is being insincere. That is why so much social life is exhausting.

Anne Morrow Lindbergh

✤ ✤ ✤ ✤

A KISS IS A LOVELY TRICK designed by nature to stop speech when words become superfluous.

Ingrid Bergman

✤ ✤ ✤ ✤

BEING IN POLITICS is like being a football coach. You have to be smart enough to understand the game and dumb enough to think it's important.

Eugene McCarthy

✤ ✤ ✤ ✤

A FANATIC IS ONE who can't change his mind and won't change the subject.

Winston Churchill

❧ ❧ ❧ ❧

EVERYTHING IS WORTH PRECISELY as much as a belch, the difference being that a belch is more satisfying.

Ingmar Bergman

❧ ❧ ❧ ❧

EVERYTHING'S GOT A MORAL, if only you can find it.

Lewis Carroll

❧ ❧ ❧ ❧

ECONOMICS IS ALL about how people make choices. Sociology is all about why they don't have any choices to make.

James S. Duesenberry

❧ ❧ ❧ ❧

THE ONLY WAY to discover the limits of the possible is to go beyond them to the impossible.

Arthur C. Clarke

❧ ❧ ❧ ❧

BUT MEN NEVER violate the laws of God without suffering the consequences, sooner or later.

Lydia M. Child

❧ ❧ ❧ ❧

DOGS COME WHEN they are called; cats take a message and get back to you.

Mary Bly

❖ ❖ ❖ ❖

NO MAN'S KNOWLEDGE here can go beyond his experience.

John Locke

❖ ❖ ❖ ❖

THE TROUBLE with the rat race is that even if you win, you're still a rat.

Lily Tomlin

❖ ❖ ❖ ❖

YOU'RE NOT OBLIGATED to win. You're obligated to keep trying to do the best you can every day.

Marian Wright Edelman

❖ ❖ ❖ ❖

I SHALL CONTINUE to be an impossible person so long as those who are now possible remain possible.

Michael Bakunin

❖ ❖ ❖ ❖

I DON'T WAIT FOR MOODS. You accomplish nothing if you do that. Your mind must know it has got to get down to work.

Pearl Buck

❖ ❖ ❖ ❖

THERE IS NO TRAP so deadly as the trap you set for yourself.

Raymond Chandler

❖ ❖ ❖ ❖

THE CHAPTER OF KNOWLEDGE is very short, but the chapter of accidents is a very long one.

Philip Dormer Stanhope (Lord Chesterfield)

❖ ❖ ❖ ❖

WE HAVE NOT THE REVERENT feeling for the rainbow that a savage has, because we know how it is made. We have lost as much as we gained by prying into that matter.

Mark Twain

❖ ❖ ❖ ❖

IF I COULD THINK that I had sent a spark to those who come after I should be ready to say Goodbye.

Oliver Wendell Holmes

❖ ❖ ❖ ❖

OUR NATIONAL DRUG is alcohol. We tend to regard the use of any other drug with special horror.

William S. Burroughs

❖ ❖ ❖ ❖

EVERY MAN IS GUILTY of all the good he didn't do.

Voltaire

❖ ❖ ❖ ❖

DISILLUSION COMES only to the illusioned. One cannot be disillusioned of what one never put faith in.

Dorothy Thompson

❧ ❧ ❧ ❧

I DON'T BELIEVE IN FAILURE. It is not failure if you enjoyed the process.

Oprah Winfrey

❧ ❧ ❧ ❧

INSANITY IS DOING the same thing over and over again, but expecting different results.

Rita Mae Brown

❧ ❧ ❧ ❧

FREEDOM IS NEVER voluntarily given by the oppressor; it must be demanded by the oppressed.

Dr. Martin Luther King, Jr.

❧ ❧ ❧ ❧

THE OPTIMIST THINKS that this is the best of all possible worlds, and the pessimist knows it.

J. Robert Oppenheimer

❧ ❧ ❧ ❧

ALL THE UTOPIAS will come to pass only when we grow wings and all people are converted into angels.

Fyodor Dostoyevsky

❧ ❧ ❧ ❧

PEOPLE WHO SAY they don't care what people think are usually desperate to have people think they don't care what people think.

George Carlin

✤ ✤ ✤ ✤

YET IT WAS THE schoolboy who said, "Faith is believing what you know ain't so."

Mark Twain

✤ ✤ ✤ ✤

COMMON SENSE is nothing more than a deposit of prejudices laid down in the mind before you reach eighteen.

Albert Einstein

✤ ✤ ✤ ✤

I'M NOT LIVING with you. We occupy the same cage.

Tennessee Williams

✤ ✤ ✤ ✤

YOU SHOULD INVEST in a business that even a fool can run, because someday a fool will.

Warren Buffett

✤ ✤ ✤ ✤

DON'T THINK. Thinking is the enemy of creativity.... You cannot try to do things. You simply must do things.

Ray Bradbury

✤ ✤ ✤ ✤

WE SPEND OUR TIME searching for security and hate it when we get it.

John Steinbeck

❧ ❧ ❧ ❧

NEVER DOUBT THAT a small group of thoughtful, committed citizens can change the world; indeed, it is the only thing that ever has.

Margaret Mead

❧ ❧ ❧ ❧

SIR, I HAVE FOUND you an argument; but I am not obliged to find you an understanding.

Samuel Johnson

❧ ❧ ❧ ❧

A DREAM WHICH is not interpreted is like a letter which is not read.

Talmud

❧ ❧ ❧ ❧

PROGRESS IS A NICE WORD. But change is its motivator and change has its enemies.

Robert F. Kennedy

❧ ❧ ❧ ❧

STRIP AWAY THE PHONY TINSEL of Hollywood and you find the real tinsel underneath.

Oscar Levant

❧ ❧ ❧ ❧

IGNORANCE IS NO EXCUSE, it's the real thing.

Irene Peter

❧ ❧ ❧ ❧

REMEMBER THAT the most beautiful things in the world are the most useless; peacocks and lilies for instance.

John Ruskin

❧ ❧ ❧ ❧

WE ARE WHAT WE PRETEND to be, so we must be careful about what we pretend to be.

Kurt Vonnegut

❧ ❧ ❧ ❧

THE MEASURE OF A MAN'S real character is what he would do if he knew he would never be found out.

Thomas Babington Macaulay (Lord Macaulay)

❧ ❧ ❧ ❧

WHEN CHOOSING BETWEEN two evils, I always like to pick the one I've never tried before.

Mae West

❧ ❧ ❧ ❧

DEAL WITH YOURSELF as an individual worthy of respect and make everyone else deal with you the same way.

Nikki Giovanni

❧ ❧ ❧ ❧

A ROCK PILE CEASES to be a rock pile the moment a single man contemplates it, bearing within him the image of a cathedral.

Antoine de Saint-Exupéry

❧ ❧ ❧ ❧

THE STRUGGLE OF MAN against power is the struggle of memory against forgetting.

Milan Kundera

❧ ❧ ❧ ❧

GOOD WILL IS THE ONE and only asset that competition cannot undersell or destroy.

Marshall Field

❧ ❧ ❧ ❧

WHAT DOES EDUCATION often do? It makes a straight-cut ditch of a free, meandering brook.

Henry David Thoreau

❧ ❧ ❧ ❧

DON'T BE RECKLESS with other people's hearts. Don't put up with people who are reckless with yours.

Mary Schmich

❧ ❧ ❧ ❧

THERE IS ONLY ONE question which really matters: Why do bad things happen to good people?

Harold S. Kushner

❧ ❧ ❧ ❧

I AM NOT a has-been. I'm a will-be.

Lauren Bacall

❧ ❧ ❧ ❧

IF ABSOLUTE POWER corrupts absolutely, does absolute power-lessness make you pure?

Harry Shearer

❧ ❧ ❧ ❧

NEVER LEND BOOKS, for no one ever returns them. The only books I have in my library are books that other folk have lent me.

Anatole France

❧ ❧ ❧ ❧

IF LIBERTY MEANS ANYTHING at all it means the right to tell people what they do not want to hear.

George Orwell

❧ ❧ ❧ ❧

THE RIGHT TO BE HEARD does not automatically include the right to be taken seriously.

Hubert H. Humphrey

❧ ❧ ❧ ❧

EACH GENERATION WASTES a little more of the future with greed and lust for riches.

Don Marquis

❧ ❧ ❧ ❧

I'D RATHER HAVE AN INCH of dog than miles of pedigree.

Dana Burnet

❧ ❧ ❧ ❧

I HAVE FOUND OUT, in the course of a long public life, that the things I did not say never hurt me.

Calvin Coolidge

❧ ❧ ❧ ❧

HUMAN BEINGS ARE PERHAPS never more frightening than when they are convinced beyond doubt that they are right.

Laurens van der Post

❧ ❧ ❧ ❧

WE ALL LIVE with the objective of being happy; our lives are all different and yet the same.

Anne Frank

❧ ❧ ❧ ❧

ALWAYS TAKE HOLD of things by the smooth handle.

Thomas Jefferson

❧ ❧ ❧ ❧

WHAT MAKES A NATION great is not primarily its great men, but the stature of its innumerable mediocre ones.

José Ortega y Gasset

❧ ❧ ❧ ❧

I DON'T LIKE PEOPLE who have never fallen or stumbled. Their virtue is lifeless and it isn't of much value. Life hasn't revealed its beauty to them.

Boris Pasternak

❧ ❧ ❧ ❧

AN EXPERT IS A PERSON who avoids the small errors as he sweeps on to the grand fallacy.

Benjamin Stolberg

❧ ❧ ❧ ❧

THERE ARE UNIVERSES begging for Gods yet He hangs around this one looking for work.

Philip José Farmer

❧ ❧ ❧ ❧

THE TRUTH OF THE MATTER is that you always know the right thing to do. The hard part is doing it.

Norman Schwarzkopf

❧ ❧ ❧ ❧

THE ONLY PERSONS who seem to have nothing to do with the education of the children are the parents.

G. K. Chesterton

❧ ❧ ❧ ❧

SERIOUS PEOPLE HAVE few ideas. People with ideas are never serious.

Paul Valéry

❧ ❧ ❧ ❧

THE SHOE THAT FITS one person pinches another: There is no universal recipe for living.

Carl Jung

✤ ✤ ✤ ✤

THINK WRONGLY, if you please, but in all cases think for yourself.

Doris Lessing

✤ ✤ ✤ ✤

I HAVE OFTEN REPENTED speaking, but never of holding my tongue.

Xenocrates

✤ ✤ ✤ ✤

THE WHOLE of the global economy is based on supplying the cravings of two percent of the world's population.

Bill Bryson

✤ ✤ ✤ ✤

TO BE QUITE FREE one must be free to refuse.

Robert Frost

✤ ✤ ✤ ✤

WHAT DID IT MATTER where you lay once you were dead? You were dead, you were sleeping the big sleep, you were not bothered by things like that.

Raymond Chandler

✤ ✤ ✤ ✤

CARICATURE is rough truth.

George Meredith

❀ ❀ ❀ ❀

THERE IS NOTHING like staying at home for real comfort.

Jane Austen

❀ ❀ ❀ ❀

TO PRODUCE A MIGHTY BOOK, you must choose a mighty theme. No great and enduring volume can ever be written on the flea, though many there be who have tried it.

Herman Melville

❀ ❀ ❀ ❀

ALL ANIMALS, EXCEPT MAN, know that the principal business of life is to enjoy it.

Samuel Butler

❀ ❀ ❀ ❀

HUMAN LIFE IS BUT A SERIES of footnotes to a vast obscure unfinished masterpiece.

Vladimir Nabokov

❀ ❀ ❀ ❀

THE MOST SUBTLE ART, the strongest and deepest art—supreme art—is the one that does not at first allow itself to be recognized.

André Gide

❀ ❀ ❀ ❀

THE WORLD IS GOVERNED by people far different from those imagined by the public.

Benjamin Disraeli

⚜ ⚜ ⚜ ⚜

IN DREAMS, we all resemble this savage.

Friedrich Nietzsche

⚜ ⚜ ⚜ ⚜

WHEN I WAS GROWING UP, there were two things that were unpopular in my house. One was me, and the other was my guitar.

Bruce Springsteen

⚜ ⚜ ⚜ ⚜

IT TAKES an entire village to raise a child.

Anonymous

⚜ ⚜ ⚜ ⚜

WHEN WRITTEN IN CHINESE, the word "crisis" is composed of two characters. One represents danger and the other represents opportunity.

John F. Kennedy

⚜ ⚜ ⚜ ⚜

SIN IS A QUEER THING. It isn't the breaking of divine commandments. It is the breaking of one's own integrity.

D. H. Lawrence

⚜ ⚜ ⚜ ⚜

THE YOUNG MAN knows the rules, but the old man knows the exceptions.

Oliver Wendell Holmes

❧ ❧ ❧ ❧

I RESPECT FAITH, but doubt is what gets you an education.

Wilson Mizner

❧ ❧ ❧ ❧

MISQUOTATION IS, in fact, the pride and privilege of the learned. A widely read man never quotes accurately, for the rather obvious reason that he has read too widely.

Hesketh Pearson

❧ ❧ ❧ ❧

JUSTICE WITHOUT FORCE is powerless; power without justice is tyrannical.

Blaise Pascal

❧ ❧ ❧ ❧

WHEN WE ARE DREAMING ALONE, it is only a dream. When we are dreaming with others, it is the beginning of reality.

Dom Hélder Câmara

❧ ❧ ❧ ❧

IF YOU RESOLVE to give up smoking, drinking, and loving, you don't actually live longer; it just seems longer.

Clement Freud

❧ ❧ ❧ ❧

THE OLD BELIEVE EVERYTHING; the middle-aged suspect everything; the young know everything.

Oscar Wilde

❧ ❧ ❧ ❧

CHILDLESSNESS HAS MANY obvious advantages. One is that you need not spend two hundred thousand dollars to send anyone to college, or contribute a similar sum to the retirement fund of a stranger who has decided to become a pediatrician. But the principal advantage of the nonparental life-style is that on Christmas Eve, you need not be struck dumb by the three most terrifying words that the government allows to be printed on any product: "Some assembly required."

John Leo

❧ ❧ ❧ ❧

IRONY is the hygiene of the mind.

Elizabeth Bibesco

❧ ❧ ❧ ❧

IT'S NOT ENOUGH to succeed. Others must fail.

Gore Vidal

❧ ❧ ❧ ❧

FIND YOUR PLACE on the planet. Dig in, and take responsibility from there.

Gary Snyder

❧ ❧ ❧ ❧

SILENCE IS THE MOST perfect expression of scorn.

George Bernard Shaw

❖ ❖ ❖ ❖

YOU CAN'T HOLD A MAN down without staying down with him.

Booker T. Washington

❖ ❖ ❖ ❖

TRUTH IS STRANGER than Fiction, but it is because Fiction is obliged to stick to possibilities; Truth isn't.

Mark Twain

❖ ❖ ❖ ❖

HUMAN BEINGS, who are almost unique in having the ability to learn from the experience of others, are also remarkable for their apparent disinclination to do so.

Douglas Adams

❖ ❖ ❖ ❖

I SWEAR . . . if you existed I'd divorce you.

Edward Albee

❖ ❖ ❖ ❖

PUBLISHING A VOLUME of verse is like dropping a rose petal down the Grand Canyon and waiting for the echo.

Don Marquis

❖ ❖ ❖ ❖

BOTH OPTIMISTS AND PESSIMISTS contribute to our society. The optimist invents the airplane and the pessimist the parachute.

Gladys Bronwyn Stern

❖ ❖ ❖ ❖

WE ARE ALL WORMS. But I do believe that I am a glowworm.

Winston Churchill

❖ ❖ ❖ ❖

THERE'S ONLY ONE REAL SIN, and that is to persuade oneself that the second-best is anything but the second-best.

Doris Lessing

❖ ❖ ❖ ❖

THE ONLY THINGS worth learning are the things you learn after you know it all.

Harry S. Truman

❖ ❖ ❖ ❖

SPORTS DO NOT BUILD character. They reveal it.

Heywood Broun

❖ ❖ ❖ ❖

ORIGINS ARE OF THE GREATEST importance. We are almost reconciled to having a cold when we remember where we caught it.

Marie von Ebner-Eschenbach

❖ ❖ ❖ ❖

INTEGRITY IS NOT a conditional word. It doesn't blow in the wind or change with the weather. It is your inner image of yourself, and if you look in there and see a man who won't cheat, then you know he never will.

John D. MacDonald

🙣 🙣 🙣 🙣

WE'RE ALL in this alone.

Lily Tomlin

🙣 🙣 🙣 🙣

TRUTH, WHEN NOT sought after, rarely comes to light.

Oliver Wendell Holmes

🙣 🙣 🙣 🙣

THE TRUE MEASURE of a man is how he treats someone who can do him absolutely no good.

Samuel Johnson

🙣 🙣 🙣 🙣

BE THANKFUL WE'RE NOT getting all the government we're paying for.

Will Rogers

🙣 🙣 🙣 🙣

TO ENLARGE OR ILLUSTRATE this power and effect of love is to set a candle in the sun.

Robert Burton

🙣 🙣 🙣 🙣

NOTHING GREAT was ever achieved without enthusiasm.

Ralph Waldo Emerson

⚜ ⚜ ⚜ ⚜

I HAVE YET TO SEE any problem, however complicated, which, when you looked at it in the right way, did not become still more complicated.

Poul Anderson

⚜ ⚜ ⚜ ⚜

THE TRUTH IS WHAT IS, not what should be. What should be is a dirty lie.

Lenny Bruce

⚜ ⚜ ⚜ ⚜

ALL TRUTH PASSES through three stages. First, it is ridiculed. Second, it is violently opposed. Third, it is accepted as being self-evident.

Arthur Schopenhauer

⚜ ⚜ ⚜ ⚜

I AM NOT DEEP, but I am very wide, and it takes time to walk round me.

Honoré de Balzac

⚜ ⚜ ⚜ ⚜

THE LIGHT of a whole life dies
When love is gone.

F. W. Bourdillon

⚜ ⚜ ⚜ ⚜

WHEN I STEPPED OUT into the bright sunlight from the darkness of the movie house, I had only two things on my mind: Paul Newman and a ride home.

S. E. Hinton

❖ ❖ ❖ ❖

FACTS DO NOT CEASE to exist because they are ignored.

Aldous Huxley

❖ ❖ ❖ ❖

LIFE IS THE ART of drawing sufficient conclusions from insufficient premises.

Samuel Butler

❖ ❖ ❖ ❖

I THINK YOU ARE WRONG to want a heart. It makes most people unhappy.

The Wizard of Oz (L. Frank Baum)

❖ ❖ ❖ ❖

THE MOST EXCITING PHRASE to hear in science, the one that heralds new discoveries, is not "Eureka!" (I found it!) but "That's funny…"

Isaac Asimov

❖ ❖ ❖ ❖

EVERY ACTIVE FORCE produces more than one change—every cause produces more than one effect.

Herbert Spencer

❖ ❖ ❖ ❖

LET US BE THANKFUL for the fools. But for them the rest of us could not succeed.

Mark Twain

❧ ❧ ❧ ❧

WHEN I USE A WORD, it means just what I choose it to mean—neither more nor less... The question is, which is to be master—that's all. They've a temper, some of them—particularly verbs, they're the proudest—adjectives you can do anything with, but not verbs. However, I can manage the whole lot of them! Impenetrability! That's what I say.

Humpty Dumpty (Lewis Carroll)

❧ ❧ ❧ ❧

SKEPTICISM is the first step towards truth.

Denis Diderot

❧ ❧ ❧ ❧

RHYTHM IS SOMETHING you either have or don't have, but when you have it you have it all over.

Elvis Presley

❧ ❧ ❧ ❧

SMALL THINGS amuse small minds.

Doris Lessing

❧ ❧ ❧ ❧

THE ART OF LOSING isn't hard to master.

Elizabeth Bishop

❧ ❧ ❧ ❧

WE MUST BE WILLING to pay a price for freedom, for no price that is ever asked for it is half the cost of doing without it.

H. L. Mencken

❧ ❧ ❧ ❧

HUMAN BEINGS are the only creatures on earth that allow their children to come back home.

Bill Cosby

❧ ❧ ❧ ❧

DOUBT IS NOT a pleasant condition, but certainty is absurd.

Voltaire

❧ ❧ ❧ ❧

POLITICS IS THE ART of preventing people from taking part in affairs which properly concern them.

Paul Valéry

❧ ❧ ❧ ❧

TOO LONG A SACRIFICE can make a stone of the heart.

William Butler Yeats

❧ ❧ ❧ ❧

THE ORIGINAL WRITER is not he who refrains from imitating others, but he who can be imitated by none.

François-René de Chateaubriand

❧ ❧ ❧ ❧

BELIEVE THAT LIFE is worth living, and your belief will help create the fact.

William James

❧ ❧ ❧ ❧

IT TAKES TIME for the absent to assume their true shape in our thoughts. After death they take on a firmer outline and then cease to change.

Colette

❧ ❧ ❧ ❧

AND AFTER ALL, what is a lie? 'Tis but the truth in masquerade.

George Gordon, Lord Byron

❧ ❧ ❧ ❧

I HAVE A THEORY that the truth is never told during the nine-to-five hours.

Hunter S. Thompson

❧ ❧ ❧ ❧

NO SOONER DO WE THINK we have assembled a comfortable life than we find a piece of ourselves that has no place to fit in.

Gail Sheehy

❧ ❧ ❧ ❧

A MAN OF GENIUS makes no mistakes. His errors are volitional and are the portals of discovery.

James Joyce

❧ ❧ ❧ ❧

WRITERS WRITE TO INFLUENCE their readers, their preachers, their auditors, but always, at bottom, to be more themselves.

Aldous Huxley

⚜ ⚜ ⚜ ⚜

WHETHER YOU THINK that you can, or that you can't, you are usually right.

Henry Ford

⚜ ⚜ ⚜ ⚜

FORTUNE KNOCKS BUT ONCE, but misfortune has much more patience.

Laurence J. Peter

⚜ ⚜ ⚜ ⚜

AN ERROR CAN NEVER become true however many times you repeat it. The truth can never be wrong, even if no one hears it.

Mohandas Gandhi

⚜ ⚜ ⚜ ⚜

ONLY A LIFE LIVED for others is a life worth living.

Albert Einstein

⚜ ⚜ ⚜ ⚜

THE NUMBER OF PEOPLE in possession of any criteria for discriminating between good and evil is very small.

T. S. Eliot

⚜ ⚜ ⚜ ⚜

I'M NOT AFRAID TO DIE. I just don't want to be there when it happens.

Woody Allen

❧ ❧ ❧ ❧

WE ARE ALL VISITORS to this time, this place. We are just passing through. Our purpose here is to observe, to learn, to grow, to love... and then we return home.

Australian Aboriginal proverb

❧ ❧ ❧ ❧

NOTHING BEFALLS A MAN except what is in his nature to endure.

Marcus Aurelius

❧ ❧ ❧ ❧

I TELL YOU, there is such a thing as creative hate!

Willa Cather

❧ ❧ ❧ ❧

ALWAYS REMEMBER that you are absolutely unique. Just like everyone else.

Margaret Mead

❧ ❧ ❧ ❧

REMEMBER THAT AS A TEENAGER you are at the last stage in your life when you will be happy to hear that the phone is for you.

Fran Lebowitz

❧ ❧ ❧ ❧

MEN HAVE BECOME the tools of their tools.

Henry David Thoreau

⚜ ⚜ ⚜ ⚜

EACH HAD HIS PAST shut in him like the leaves of a book known to him by heart; and his friends could only read the title.

Virginia Woolf

⚜ ⚜ ⚜ ⚜

WHEN YOU STEP ON A SNAKE or brush against it, its venom can kill you. But a slanderer's venom is of another type entirely—it enters one person's ear, yet destroys another.

Sanskrit verse

⚜ ⚜ ⚜ ⚜

BREVITY is the sister of talent.

Anton Chekhov

⚜ ⚜ ⚜ ⚜

WHENEVER I DATE A GUY, I think, is this the man I want my children to spend their weekends with?

Rita Rudner

⚜ ⚜ ⚜ ⚜

AN INFALLIBLE METHOD of conciliating a tiger is to allow oneself to be devoured.

Konrad Adenauer

⚜ ⚜ ⚜ ⚜

WE KNOW THAT THE NATURE of genius is to provide idiots with ideas twenty years later.

Louis Aragon

❧ ❧ ❧ ❧

THE PRACTICE OF VIOLENCE, like all action, changes the world, but the most probable change is to a more violent world.

Hannah Arendt

❧ ❧ ❧ ❧

OURS IS A WORLD where people don't know what they want and are willing to go through hell to get it.

Don Marquis

❧ ❧ ❧ ❧

THE ONLY MAN who wasn't spoilt by being lionized was Daniel.

Herbert Beerbohm Tree

❧ ❧ ❧ ❧

TO BE A CHAMPION, you have to believe in yourself when nobody else will.

Sugar Ray Robinson

❧ ❧ ❧ ❧

IT REQUIRES WISDOM to understand wisdom; the music is nothing if the audience is deaf.

Walter Lippmann

❧ ❧ ❧ ❧

THE AIM OF LIFE is life itself.

Johann Wolfgang von Goethe

❖ ❖ ❖ ❖

COURAGE IS ALMOST a contradiction in terms. It means a strong desire to live taking the form of a readiness to die.

G. K. Chesterton

❖ ❖ ❖ ❖

THERE IS NO DUTY we so much underrate as the duty of being happy.

Robert Louis Stevenson

❖ ❖ ❖ ❖

CATS SEEM TO GO on the principle that it never does any harm to ask for what you want.

Joseph Wood Krutch

❖ ❖ ❖ ❖

IF YOU ARE TOO CAREFUL, you are so occupied in being careful that you are sure to stumble over something.

Gertrude Stein

❖ ❖ ❖ ❖

THE ONLY THING that saves us from the bureaucracy is inefficiency. An efficient bureaucracy is the greatest threat to liberty.

Eugene McCarthy

❖ ❖ ❖ ❖

A FELLOW WHO is always declaring he's no fool usually has his suspicions.

Wilson Mizner

❧ ❧ ❧ ❧

FEW TASKS ARE MORE LIKE the torture of Sisyphus than housework, with its endless repetition.... The housewife wears herself out marking time: She makes nothing, simply perpetuates the present.

Simone de Beauvoir

❧ ❧ ❧ ❧

I AM A MAN OF FIXED and unbending principles, the first of which is to be flexible at all times.

Everett Dirksen

❧ ❧ ❧ ❧

THE MORE YOU LET yourself go, the less others let you go.

Friedrich Nietzsche

❧ ❧ ❧ ❧

I ALWAYS LOVE to quote Albert Einstein because nobody dares contradict him.

Studs Terkel

❧ ❧ ❧ ❧

A MAN CAN DO ONLY what he can do. But if he does that each day he can sleep at night and do it again the next day.

Dr. Albert Schweitzer

❧ ❧ ❧ ❧

THERE IS NO SAFETY for honest men, but by believing all possible evil of evil men.

Edmund Burke

COLLEGE ISN'T THE PLACE to go for ideas.

Helen Keller

I AWOKE ONE MORNING and found myself famous.

George Gordon, Lord Byron

THE QUESTION FOR EACH MAN to settle is not what he would do if he had the means, time, influence and educational advantages, but what he will do with the things he has.

Hamilton Wright Mabee

IN THIS WORLD we run the risk of having to choose between being either the anvil or the hammer.

Voltaire

THE BETTER WE FEEL about ourselves, the fewer times we have to knock somebody else down to feel tall.

Odetta

ONE SHORT SLEEP PAST, we wake eternally,
And death shall be no more; Death, thou shalt die.

John Donne

❧ ❧ ❧ ❧

I WOULDN'T DESCRIBE myself as lacking in confidence, but I
would just say that the ghosts you chase you never catch.

John Malkovich

❧ ❧ ❧ ❧

I DON'T LOVE STUDYING. I hate studying. I like learning. Learning is beautiful.

Natalie Portman

❧ ❧ ❧ ❧

I HAVE LOST FRIENDS, some by death . . . others through sheer
inability to cross the street.

Virginia Woolf

❧ ❧ ❧ ❧

IF EVERYBODY'S THINKING the same thing, then nobody's
thinking.

George S. Patton

❧ ❧ ❧ ❧

WHATEVER EXISTS at all exists in some amount. To know it
thoroughly involves knowing its quantity as well as its quality.

Edward L. Thorndike

❧ ❧ ❧ ❧

GENIUS IS DIVINE PERSEVERANCE. Genius I cannot claim nor even extra brightness, but perseverance all can have.

Woodrow Wilson

⚜ ⚜ ⚜ ⚜

THE VERY LEAST YOU CAN DO in your life is to figure out what you hope for. And the most you can do is live inside that hope.

Barbara Kingsolver

⚜ ⚜ ⚜ ⚜

COURAGE is grace under pressure.

Ernest Hemingway

⚜ ⚜ ⚜ ⚜

OUR GREATEST PRETENSES are built up not to hide the evil and the ugly in us, but our emptiness. The hardest thing to hide is something that is not there.

Eric Hoffer

⚜ ⚜ ⚜ ⚜

WINNING MAY NOT BE EVERYTHING, but losing has little to recommend it.

Dianne Feinstein

⚜ ⚜ ⚜ ⚜

NO ONE ON HIS DEATHBED ever said, "I wish I had spent more time on my business."

Arnold Zack

⚜ ⚜ ⚜ ⚜

CRITICISM IS EASY, art is difficult.

Philippe Destouches

❧ ❧ ❧ ❧

THERE ARE TRUTHS which one can only say after having won the right to say them.

Jean Cocteau

❧ ❧ ❧ ❧

FIND OUT WHO YOU ARE and do it on purpose.

Dolly Parton

❧ ❧ ❧ ❧

YOU WILL KNOW your enemies because they are the ones that interfere with the work.

Bette Davis

❧ ❧ ❧ ❧

THE BEST WE CAN DO is be kindly and helpful toward our friends and fellow passengers who are clinging to the same speck of dirt while we are drifting side by side to our common doom.

Clarence Darrow

❧ ❧ ❧ ❧

BUY LAND. They're not making it anymore.

Mark Twain

❧ ❧ ❧ ❧

BY THE TIME A MAN realizes that maybe his father was right, he usually has a son who thinks he's wrong.

Charles Wadsworth

❧ ❧ ❧ ❧

TIME IS THE COIN of your life. It is the only coin you have, and only you can determine how it will be spent. Be careful lest you let other people spend it for you.

Carl Sandburg

❧ ❧ ❧ ❧

BE AS YOU ARE and hope that it's right.

Dizzy Gillespie

❧ ❧ ❧ ❧

THE DEGREE OF CIVILIZATION in a society can be judged by entering its prisons.

Fyodor Dostoyevsky

❧ ❧ ❧ ❧

MAN IS SO MADE that he can only find relaxation from one kind of labor by taking up another.

Anatole France

❧ ❧ ❧ ❧

WHAT ONE KNOWS IS, in youth, of little moment; they know enough who know how to learn.

Henry Adams

❧ ❧ ❧ ❧

WE ARE ALWAYS the same age inside.

Gertrude Stein

❧ ❧ ❧ ❧

THROUGH THE THOU a person becomes I.

Martin Buber

❧ ❧ ❧ ❧

THE ANT, WHO HAS TOILED and dragged a crumb to his nest, will furiously defend the fruit of his labor, against whatever robber assails him. So plain, that the most dumb and stupid slave that ever toiled for a master, does constantly know that he is wronged. So plain that no one, high or low, ever does mistake it, except in a plainly selfish way; for although volume upon volume is written to prove slavery a very good thing, we never hear of the man who wishes to take the good of it, by being a slave himself.

Abraham Lincoln

❧ ❧ ❧ ❧

THERE IS A SKELETON in every house.

William Makepeace Thackeray

❧ ❧ ❧ ❧

KEEP UP THE GOOD WORK, if only for a while, if only for the twinkling of a tiny galaxy.

Wislawa Symborska

❧ ❧ ❧ ❧

THE END OF THE HUMAN RACE will be that it will eventually die of civilization.

Ralph Waldo Emerson

❧ ❧ ❧ ❧

I HOLD THIS TO BE the highest task for a bond between two people: that each protects the solitude of the other.

Rainer Maria Rilke

❧ ❧ ❧ ❧

HAPPINESS OFTEN SNEAKS in through a door you didn't know you left open.

John Barrymore

❧ ❧ ❧ ❧

THE MOST FUN in breaking a rule is in knowing what rule you're breaking.

William Safire

❧ ❧ ❧ ❧

I CAN NEVER READ all the books I want; I can never be all the people I want and live all the lives I want.

Sylvia Plath

❧ ❧ ❧ ❧

BEHOLD THE TURTLE. He makes progress only when he sticks his neck out.

James Bryant Conant

❧ ❧ ❧ ❧

THERE IS NOT A DREAM which may not come true, if we have the energy which makes or chooses our own fate.... It is only the dreams of those light sleepers who dream faintly that do not come true.

Arthur Symons

⚜ ⚜ ⚜ ⚜

I AM somebody!

Jesse Jackson

⚜ ⚜ ⚜ ⚜

BOTH THE COCKROACH and the bird could get along very well without us, although the cockroach would miss us most.

Joseph Wood Krutch

⚜ ⚜ ⚜ ⚜

THERE IS NOTHING IMPOSSIBLE, therefore, in the existence of the supernatural; its existence seems to me decidedly probable; there is infinite room for it on every side.

George Santayana

⚜ ⚜ ⚜ ⚜

REALITY IS WRONG. Dreams are for real.

Tupac Shakur

⚜ ⚜ ⚜ ⚜

A TENDENCY TO FLY too straight at a goal, instead of circling around it, often carries one too far.

Lin Yutang

⚜ ⚜ ⚜ ⚜

IF YOU CANNOT INSPIRE a woman with love of you, fill her above the brim with love of herself; all that runs over will be yours.

Charles Caleb Colton

✦ ✦ ✦ ✦

IF COLUMBUS HAD an advisory committee, he would probably still be at the dock.

Arthur Goldberg

✦ ✦ ✦ ✦

MOST PEOPLE WOULD sooner die than think. In fact, they do so.

Bertrand Russell

✦ ✦ ✦ ✦

THE LAST THING one knows in constructing a work is what to put first.

Blaise Pascal

✦ ✦ ✦ ✦

JUST REMEMBER, once you're over the hill, you begin to pick up speed.

Charles Schulz

✦ ✦ ✦ ✦

THE THING THAT'S IMPORTANT to know is that you never know. You're always sort of feeling your way.

Diane Arbus

✦ ✦ ✦ ✦

THERE IS NO MORE expensive thing than a free gift.

Michel de Montaigne

❧ ❧ ❧ ❧

FOOTBALL IS NOT A CONTACT SPORT; it's a collision sport. Dancing is a good example of a contact sport.

Hugh "Duffy" Daugherty

❧ ❧ ❧ ❧

WISDOM DOESN'T automatically come with old age. Nothing does—except wrinkles. It's true, some wines improve with age. But only if the grapes were good in the first place.

Abigail Van Buren

❧ ❧ ❧ ❧

JAZZ WAS LIKE the kind of man you wouldn't want your daughter to associate with.

Duke Ellington

❧ ❧ ❧ ❧

BLESSED IS HE who expects nothing, for he shall never be disappointed.

Jonathan Swift

❧ ❧ ❧ ❧

CHILDHOOD is the kingdom where nobody dies.

Edna St. Vincent Millay

❧ ❧ ❧ ❧

ALL WARFARE is based on deception.

Sun Tzu

❧ ❧ ❧ ❧

WHAT AMERICA NEEDS most today is what it once had, but has lost: the lift of a driving dream.

Richard Nixon

❧ ❧ ❧ ❧

THE PROBLEM with the gene pool is that there is no lifeguard.

Steven Wright

❧ ❧ ❧ ❧

I PAINT MY OWN REALITY. The only thing I know is that I paint because I need to, and I paint whatever passes through my head without any other consideration.

Frida Kahlo

❧ ❧ ❧ ❧

LIFE DOES NOT CEASE to be funny when people die any more than it ceases to be serious when people laugh.

George Bernard Shaw

❧ ❧ ❧ ❧

MEN NEVER DO EVIL so completely and cheerfully as when they do it from religious conviction.

Blaise Pascal

❧ ❧ ❧ ❧

YOUR MOST UNHAPPY CUSTOMERS are your greatest source of learning.

Bill Gates

❧ ❧ ❧ ❧

NO MEMORY IS EVER ALONE; it's at the end of a trail of memories, a dozen trails that each have their own associations.

Louis L'Amour

❧ ❧ ❧ ❧

THE ONLY REASON people want to be masters of the future is to change the past.

Milan Kundera

❧ ❧ ❧ ❧

SENTENCE FIRST—verdict afterwards.

Lewis Carroll

❧ ❧ ❧ ❧

AN UNCONDITIONAL RIGHT to say what one pleases about public affairs is what I consider to be the minimum guarantee of the First Amendment.

Hugo L. Black

❧ ❧ ❧ ❧

A MOTHER IS NOT a person to lean on but a person to make leaning unnecessary.

Dorothy Canfield Fisher

❧ ❧ ❧ ❧

GLORY IS FLEETING, but obscurity is forever.

Napoléon Bonaparte

❀ ❀ ❀ ❀

HOW WOULD MAN EXIST if God did not need him, and how would you exist? You need God in order to be, and God needs you—for that is the meaning of life.

Martin Buber

❀ ❀ ❀ ❀

SOME SAY THE WORLD will end in fire,
Some say in ice.

Robert Frost

❀ ❀ ❀ ❀

IT IS BETTER TO KNOW some of the questions than all of the answers.

James Thurber

❀ ❀ ❀ ❀

SOMETIMES YOUR BEST investments are the ones you don't make.

Donald Trump

❀ ❀ ❀ ❀

WHEN WE CANNOT BEAR to be alone, it means we do not properly value the only companion we will have from birth to death—ourselves.

Eda LeShan

❀ ❀ ❀ ❀

BEING ENTIRELY HONEST with oneself is a good exercise.

Sigmund Freud

⚜ ⚜ ⚜ ⚜

LIFE IS LIKE Sanskrit read to a pony.

Lou Reed

⚜ ⚜ ⚜ ⚜

THE MEDIA ARE NOT TOYS; they should not be in the hands of Mother Goose and Peter Pan executives. They can be entrusted only to new artists, because they are art forms.

Marshall McLuhan

⚜ ⚜ ⚜ ⚜

YOU'RE EITHER on the bus or off the bus.

Ken Kesey

⚜ ⚜ ⚜ ⚜

IT IS A PARADOX that as we reach our prime, we also see there is a place where it finishes.

Gail Sheehy

⚜ ⚜ ⚜ ⚜

INFORMATION IS NOT POWER. If information were power, then librarians would be the most powerful people on the planet.

Bruce Sterling

⚜ ⚜ ⚜ ⚜

MAN IS AN INTELLIGENCE, not served by, but in servitude to his organs.

Aldous Huxley

❧ ❧ ❧ ❧

THE INDISPENSABLE FIRST STEP to getting the things you want out of life is this: Decide what you want.

Ben Stein

❧ ❧ ❧ ❧

SOME MAY NEVER LIVE, but the crazy never die.

Hunter S. Thompson

❧ ❧ ❧ ❧

IT IS QUITE TRUE what Philosophy says: that Life must be understood backwards. But that makes one forget the other saying: that it must be lived—forwards.

Søren Kierkegaard

❧ ❧ ❧ ❧

THE CURE FOR BOREDOM is curiosity. There is no cure for curiosity.

Dorothy Parker

❧ ❧ ❧ ❧

NOT A SHRED OF EVIDENCE exists in favor of the idea that life is serious.

Brendan Gill

❧ ❧ ❧ ❧

EVERY MAN'S LIFE ENDS the same way, and it is only the details of how he lived and how he died that distinguishes one man from another.

Ernest Hemingway

✤ ✤ ✤ ✤

HISTORY, DESPITE ITS wrenching pain, cannot be unlived, but if faced with courage, need not be lived again.

Maya Angelou

✤ ✤ ✤ ✤

BE NICE TO PEOPLE on your way up, because you'll meet them on your way down.

Wilson Mizner

✤ ✤ ✤ ✤

EVERYONE IS BORN a genius, but the process of living de-geniuses them.

Buckminster Fuller

✤ ✤ ✤ ✤

IN THE LEXICON OF YOUTH, which fate reserves for a bright manhood, there is no such word as "fail."

Edward George Bulwer-Lytton

✤ ✤ ✤ ✤

IDEAS ARE MORE POWERFUL than guns. We would not let our enemies have guns—why should we let them have ideas?

Franz Werfel

✤ ✤ ✤ ✤

COMPASSION IS THE ANTITOXIN of the soul: Where there is compassion, even the most poisonous impulses remain relatively harmless.

Eric Hoffer

✿ ✿ ✿ ✿

IN THE FUTURE, everybody will be world-famous for fifteen minutes.

Andy Warhol

✿ ✿ ✿ ✿

THE FOOT FEELS the foot when it feels the ground.

Buddha

✿ ✿ ✿ ✿

ALL HISTORY SHOWS that the hand that cradles the rock has ruled the world, not the hand that rocks the cradle!

Clare Boothe Luce

✿ ✿ ✿ ✿

NO PAIN, NO PALM; no thorns, no throne; no gall, no glory; no cross, no crown.

William Penn

✿ ✿ ✿ ✿

NO SADDER PROOF can be given by a man of his own littleness than disbelief in great men.

Thomas Carlyle

✿ ✿ ✿ ✿

EDUCATION IS WHAT SURVIVES when what has been learnt has been forgotten.

B. F. Skinner

❧ ❧ ❧ ❧

THE STRUGGLE TO REACH the top is itself enough to fulfill the heart of man. One must believe that Sisyphus is happy.

Albert Camus

❧ ❧ ❧ ❧

CIVIL DISOBEDIENCE becomes a sacred duty when the State becomes lawless or, which is the same thing, corrupt.

Mohandas Gandhi

❧ ❧ ❧ ❧

A MAN'S DYING is more the survivors' affair than his own.

Thomas Mann

❧ ❧ ❧ ❧

CHILDREN'S GAMES are hardly games. Children are never more serious than when they play.

Michel de Montaigne

❧ ❧ ❧ ❧

EXCEPT FOR THE OCCASIONAL heart attack, I feel as young as I ever did.

Robert Benchley

❧ ❧ ❧ ❧

LIFE IS FAR TOO IMPORTANT a thing ever to talk seriously about.

Oscar Wilde

❧ ❧ ❧ ❧

TO FINISH A PICTURE? What nonsense! To finish it means to be through with it, to kill it, to rid it of its soul, to give it its final blow.

Pablo Picasso

❧ ❧ ❧ ❧

NO ONE CAN ARRIVE from being talented alone. God gives talent; work transforms talent into genius.

Anna Pavlova

❧ ❧ ❧ ❧

A COMEDIAN DOES FUNNY THINGS. A good comedian does things funny.

Buster Keaton

❧ ❧ ❧ ❧

THE REALLY FRIGHTENING thing about middle age is the knowledge that you'll grow out of it.

Doris Day

❧ ❧ ❧ ❧

WHEN IDEAS FAIL, a word comes in to save the situation.

Johann Wolfgang von Goethe

❧ ❧ ❧ ❧

I AM A RED MAN. If the Great Spirit had desired me to be a white man he would have made me so in the first place. He put in your heart certain wishes and plans, in my heart he put other and different desires. Each man is good in his sight. It is not necessary for Eagles to be Crows. We are poor, but we are free.

Sitting Bull

❧ ❧ ❧ ❧

THE LIFE WHICH is unexamined is not worth living.

Plato

❧ ❧ ❧ ❧

ALMOST EVERY WISE SAYING has an opposite one, no less wise, to balance it.

George Santayana

❧ ❧ ❧ ❧

ONE IS ALWAYS at home in one's past.

Vladimir Nabokov

❧ ❧ ❧ ❧

TIME IS THE SCHOOL in which we learn,
Time is the fire in which we burn.

Delmore Schwartz

❧ ❧ ❧ ❧

FAME is a powerful aphrodisiac.

Graham Greene

❧ ❧ ❧ ❧

ONE CAN NEVER consent to creep when one feels an impulse to soar.

Helen Keller

❧ ❧ ❧ ❧

OF TWO FRIENDS, one is always the other's slave.

Mikhail Lermontov

❧ ❧ ❧ ❧

HE WHO DOES NOT GET FUN and enjoyment out of every day needs to reorganize his life.

George M. Adams

❧ ❧ ❧ ❧

LIFE IS POSSESSED by everybody from the garden worm up. It exists because the creator of this universe wanted it to exist. He designed it so it would perpetuate itself.

William Westmoreland

❧ ❧ ❧ ❧

ORIGINAL THOUGHT is like original sin: Both happened before you were born to people you could not have possibly met.

Fran Lebowitz

❧ ❧ ❧ ❧

REVOLUTION BEGINS with the self, in the self.

Toni Cade Bambara

❧ ❧ ❧ ❧

ALL THINGS truly wicked start from innocence.

Ernest Hemingway

❧ ❧ ❧ ❧

IF I SHOULD MEET THEE,
After long years,
How should I greet thee?—
With silence and tears.

George Gordon, Lord Byron

❧ ❧ ❧ ❧

MY GRANDFATHER ONCE told me that there were two kinds of people: those who do the work and those who take the credit. He told me to try to be in the first group; there was much less competition.

Indira Gandhi

❧ ❧ ❧ ❧

THAT'S ALWAYS THE WAY when you discover something new: Everybody thinks you're crazy.

Evelyn E. Smith

❧ ❧ ❧ ❧

ONE DOES WHAT ONE IS; one becomes what one does.

Robert von Musil

❧ ❧ ❧ ❧

MORAL INDIGNATION is jealousy with a halo.

H. G. Wells

❧ ❧ ❧ ❧

WE ALL WEAR MASKS, and the time comes when we cannot remove them without removing some of our own skin.

André Berthiaume

❖ ❖ ❖ ❖

AN EPIGRAM IS ONLY a wisecrack that's played Carnegie Hall.

Oscar Levant

❖ ❖ ❖ ❖

I WANT TO REACH THAT STATE of condensation of sensations which constitutes a picture.

Henri Matisse

❖ ❖ ❖ ❖

IT REQUIRES A VERY UNUSUAL MIND to undertake the analysis of the obvious.

Alfred North Whitehead

❖ ❖ ❖ ❖

THERE ARE TWO WAYS of exerting one's strength: One is pushing down; the other is pulling up.

Booker T. Washington

❖ ❖ ❖ ❖

IRRESPONSIBILITY IS PART of the pleasure of all art; it is the part the schools cannot recognize.

Pauline Kael

❖ ❖ ❖ ❖

LOVE IS ALL WE HAVE, the only way that each can help the other.

Euripides

❦ ❦ ❦ ❦

IT IS EASIER to denature plutonium than to denature the evil spirit of man.

Albert Einstein

❦ ❦ ❦ ❦

AS THE ARCHAEOLOGY of our thought easily shows, man is an invention of recent date. And one perhaps nearing its end.

Michel Foucault

❦ ❦ ❦ ❦

A SYNONYM IS A WORD you use when you can't spell the word you first thought of.

Burt Bacharach

❦ ❦ ❦ ❦

IT TAKES FIVE HUNDRED small details to add up to one favorable impression.

Cary Grant

❦ ❦ ❦ ❦

THE JOY THAT ISN'T SHARED dies young.

Anne Sexton

❦ ❦ ❦ ❦

THERE IS NO EXCEPTION to the rule that every rule has an exception.

James Thurber

❧ ❧ ❧ ❧

NOTHING IS MORE DESIRABLE than to be released from an affliction, but nothing is more frightening than to be divested of a crutch.

James Baldwin

❧ ❧ ❧ ❧

NATURE MAKES NOTHING incomplete, and nothing in vain.

Aristotle

❧ ❧ ❧ ❧

IMAGINATION IS THE BEGINNING of creation. You imagine what you desire; you will what you imagine; and at last you create what you will.

George Bernard Shaw

❧ ❧ ❧ ❧

I DON'T WANT EVERYONE to like me; I should think less of myself if some people did.

Henry James

❧ ❧ ❧ ❧

ARGUE FOR YOUR LIMITATIONS, and sure enough, they're yours.

Richard Bach

❧ ❧ ❧ ❧

FEW THINGS ARE HARDER to put up with than the annoyance of a good example.

Mark Twain

❖ ❖ ❖ ❖

HE WHO KNOWS does not speak. He who speaks does not know.

Lao Tzu

❖ ❖ ❖ ❖

YOU CANNOT PREVENT the birds of sadness from flying over your head, but you can prevent them from nesting in your hair.

Chinese proverb

❖ ❖ ❖ ❖

YOU SEE, but you do not observe.

Sir Arthur Conan Doyle

❖ ❖ ❖ ❖

MIRACLES ARE INSTANTANEOUS, they cannot be summoned, but come of themselves, usually at unlikely moments and to those who least expect them.

Katherine Anne Porter

❖ ❖ ❖ ❖

IF YOU TREAT EVERY SITUATION as a life-and-death matter, you'll die a lot of times.

Dean Smith

❖ ❖ ❖ ❖

OUT BEYOND IDEAS of wrongdoing and rightdoing, there is a field. I will meet you there.

Jalal ad-Din Rumi

❧ ❧ ❧ ❧

THE PAST IS NEVER DEAD. It's not even past.

William Faulkner

❧ ❧ ❧ ❧

HOW LONG WILL the human race sweat under the superstition that, in order to be happy and useful and intelligent, it is necessary to believe in things? What nonsense indeed! Human progress consists, not in acquiring beliefs, but in getting rid of them.

H. L. Mencken

❧ ❧ ❧ ❧

PEOPLE WHO DRINK to drown their sorrow should be told that sorrow knows how to swim.

Ann Landers

❧ ❧ ❧ ❧

FATE IS NOT AN EAGLE, it creeps like a rat.

Elizabeth Bowen

❧ ❧ ❧ ❧

HONESTY IS AS RARE as a man without self-pity.

Stephen Vincent Benét

❧ ❧ ❧ ❧

THE GREATEST INVENTION of the nineteenth century was the invention of the method of invention.

Alfred North Whitehead

❧ ❧ ❧ ❧

THE CHIEF OBSTACLE to the progress of the human race is the human race.

Don Marquis

❧ ❧ ❧ ❧

WHEN ACTION GROWS unprofitable, gather information; when information grows unprofitable, sleep.

Ursula K. Le Guin

❧ ❧ ❧ ❧

THE CREATIVE INDIVIDUAL has the capacity to free himself from the web of social pressures in which the rest of us are caught. He is capable of questioning the assumptions that the rest of us accept.

John W. Gardner

❧ ❧ ❧ ❧

LAW MUST BE STABLE and yet it cannot stand still.

Roscoe Pound

❧ ❧ ❧ ❧

NOTHING is permanent but change.

Heraclitus

❧ ❧ ❧ ❧

TAKE ME OR LEAVE ME; or, as is the usual order of things, both.

Dorothy Parker

❧ ❧ ❧ ❧

MY INTEREST IS IN THE FUTURE because I'm going to spend the rest of my life there.

Charles F. Kettering

❧ ❧ ❧ ❧

EVERYTHING IS DANGEROUS, my dear fellow. If it wasn't so, life wouldn't be worth living.

Oscar Wilde

❧ ❧ ❧ ❧

ONE OF THE DELIGHTS known to age, and beyond the grasp of youth, is that of Not Going.

J. B. Priestley

❧ ❧ ❧ ❧

THERE'S A HELLUVA DISTANCE between wise-cracking and wit. Wit has truth in it; wise-cracking is simply calisthenics with words.

Dorothy Parker

❧ ❧ ❧ ❧

WHY DO THEY BOTHER saying raw sewage? Do some people cook that stuff?

George Carlin

❧ ❧ ❧ ❧

NO MATTER HOW MUCH cats fight, there always seem to be plenty of kittens.

Abraham Lincoln

❧ ❧ ❧ ❧

IT'S A POOR SORT of memory that only works backwards.

Lewis Carroll

❧ ❧ ❧ ❧

THE HUMAN MIND is inspired enough when it comes to inventing horrors; it is when it tries to invent a heaven that it shows itself cloddish.

Evelyn Waugh

❧ ❧ ❧ ❧

IN TIMES LIKE THESE, it helps to recall that there have always been times like these.

Paul Harvey

❧ ❧ ❧ ❧

THERE IS ALWAYS one moment in childhood when the door opens and lets the future in.

Graham Greene

❧ ❧ ❧ ❧

A WEAK MAN has doubts before a decision; a strong man has them afterwards.

Karl Krauss

❧ ❧ ❧ ❧

THE REAL PROBLEM is what to do with the problem-solvers after the problems are solved.

Gay Talese

WELL DONE is better than well said.

Benjamin Franklin

WE DO NOT HAVE to visit a madhouse to find disordered minds; our planet is the mental institution of the universe.

Johann Wolfgang von Goethe

MAN'S MAIN TASK in life is to give birth to himself, to become what he potentially is.

Erich Fromm

THE FIRST HUMAN who hurled an insult instead of a stone was the founder of civilization.

Sigmund Freud

I THINK THERE IS ONLY one quality worse than hardness of heart, and that is softness of head.

Theodore Roosevelt

LIFE HAS TAUGHT me to think, but thinking has not taught me how to live.

Alexander Herzen

❧ ❧ ❧ ❧

THERE ARE NO hopeless situations; there are only people who have grown hopeless about them.

Clare Boothe Luce

❧ ❧ ❧ ❧

THE PATHWAY TO GLORY is rough, and many gloomy hours obscure it. May the Great Spirit shed light on yours, and that you may never experience the humility that the power of the American government has reduced me to, is the wish of him who, in his native forests, was once as proud and bold as yourself.

Black Hawk

❧ ❧ ❧ ❧

A LITTLE ALARM now and then keeps life from stagnation.

Fanny Burney

❧ ❧ ❧ ❧

LIFE IS A MAZE in which we take the wrong turning before we have learnt to walk.

Cyril Connolly

❧ ❧ ❧ ❧

THE WIND AND THE WAVES are always on the side of the ablest navigators.

Edward Gibbons

❧ ❧ ❧ ❧

WHEN YOU GET INTO a tight place and everything goes against you till it seems as if you couldn't hold on a minute longer, never give up then, for that's just the place and time that the tide'll turn.

Harriet Beecher Stowe

❧ ❧ ❧ ❧

SPEAK WHEN YOU arc angry and you will make the best speech you will ever regret.

Ambrose Bierce

❧ ❧ ❧ ❧

AS WE GROW OLD, the beauty steals inward.

Ralph Waldo Emerson

❧ ❧ ❧ ❧

THERE ARE PERSONS WHO, when they cease to shock us, cease to interest us.

F. H. Bradley

❧ ❧ ❧ ❧

GROWTH FOR THE SAKE of growth is the ideology of the cancer cell.

Edward Abbey

❧ ❧ ❧ ❧

GENIUS IS ONLY a greater aptitude for patience.

Georges-Louis Leclerc, Comte de Buffon

❧ ❧ ❧ ❧

THINGS THAT MATTER most must never be at the mercy of things that matter least.

Johann Wolfgang von Goethe

⚜ ⚜ ⚜ ⚜

THE BREAD OF LIFE is love; the salt of life is work; the sweetness of life, poesy; the water of life, faith.

Anna Jameson

⚜ ⚜ ⚜ ⚜

THE NATURE OF MEN is always the same; it is their habits that separate them.

Confucius

⚜ ⚜ ⚜ ⚜

THERE IS NOTHING new in the world except the history you do not know.

Harry S. Truman

⚜ ⚜ ⚜ ⚜

ESTABLISHING GOALS is all right if you don't let them deprive you of interesting detours.

Doug Larson

⚜ ⚜ ⚜ ⚜

CREATIVE MINDS have always been known to survive any kind of bad training.

Anna Freud

⚜ ⚜ ⚜ ⚜

THE WISEST MIND has something yet to learn.

George Santayana

❧ ❧ ❧ ❧

NOT TO TRANSMIT an experience is to betray it.

Elie Wiesel

❧ ❧ ❧ ❧

I WRITE ENTIRELY to find out what I'm thinking, what I'm looking at, what I see and what it means. What I want and what I fear.

Joan Didion

❧ ❧ ❧ ❧

IN SPITE OF EVERYTHING, I still believe that people are really good at heart. I simply can't build up my hopes on a foundation consisting of confusion, misery, and death.

Anne Frank

❧ ❧ ❧ ❧

THERE IS NO HOPE unmingled with fear, and no fear unmingled with hope.

Baruch de Spinoza

❧ ❧ ❧ ❧

TO CONQUER WITHOUT risk is to triumph without glory.

Pierre Corneille

❧ ❧ ❧ ❧

THERE ARE MANY THINGS in life more important than money. And they all cost money.

Fred Allen

❧ ❧ ❧ ❧

GREAT LITERATURE is simply language charged with meaning to the utmost possible degree.

Ezra Pound

❧ ❧ ❧ ❧

BENEATH THE RULE of men entirely great, the pen is mightier than the sword.

Edward George Bulwer-Lytton

❧ ❧ ❧ ❧

ALL HUMAN BEINGS are also dream beings. Dreaming ties all mankind together.

Jack Kerouac

❧ ❧ ❧ ❧

COURAGE IS NOT SIMPLY one of the virtues, but the form of every virtue at the testing point.

C. S. Lewis

❧ ❧ ❧ ❧

MAN IS THE ONLY creature that consumes without producing.

George Orwell

❧ ❧ ❧ ❧

WHAT IS MOST ORIGINAL in a man's nature is often that which is most desperate.

Leonard Cohen

❧ ❧ ❧ ❧

AN ECONOMIST IS AN EXPERT who will know tomorrow why the things he predicted yesterday didn't happen today.

Laurence J. Peter

❧ ❧ ❧ ❧

CATS ARE INTENDED to teach us that not everything in nature has a purpose.

Garrison Keillor

❧ ❧ ❧ ❧

NEVER CONFUSE KNOWLEDGE with wisdom. By wisdom I mean wrestling with how to live.

Cornel West

❧ ❧ ❧ ❧

WE DON'T WANT OUR BUILDINGS merely to shelter us; we also want them to speak to us.

John Ruskin

❧ ❧ ❧ ❧

DEMOCRACY IS A PROCESS by which the people are free to choose the man who will get the blame.

Laurence J. Peter

❧ ❧ ❧ ❧

OUR TRUE WEALTH is the good we do in this world. None of us has faith unless we desire for our neighbors what we desire for ourselves.

Muhammad

❖ ❖ ❖ ❖

IN ALL CHAOS there is a cosmos, in all disorder a secret order.

Carl Jung

❖ ❖ ❖ ❖

ALL BOOKS ARE EITHER dreams or swords,
You can cut, or you can drug, with words.

Amy Lowell

❖ ❖ ❖ ❖

AN EYE FOR AN EYE makes the whole world go blind.

Mohandas Gandhi

❖ ❖ ❖ ❖

PAY ATTENTION TO YOUR ENEMIES, for they are the first to discover your mistakes.

Antisthenes

❖ ❖ ❖ ❖

ANALYZING HUMOR is like dissecting a frog. Few people are interested and the frog dies of it.

E. B. White

❖ ❖ ❖ ❖

THE UNCONSCIOUS IS THE OCEAN of the unsayable, of what has been expelled from the land of language, removed as a result of ancient prohibitions.

Italo Calvino

❧ ❧ ❧ ❧

LIKE SNOWFLAKES, the human pattern is never cast twice.

Alice Childress

❧ ❧ ❧ ❧

THERE IS NO POINT at which you can say, "Well, I'm successful now. I might as well take a nap."

Carrie Fisher

❧ ❧ ❧ ❧

ALL THE TRUTH in the world adds up to one big lie.

Bob Dylan

❧ ❧ ❧ ❧

WHEN WE REMEMBER we are all mad, the mysteries disappear and life stands explained.

Mark Twain

❧ ❧ ❧ ❧

IF YOU'RE GOING to go through hell . . . I suggest you come back learning something.

Drew Barrymore

❧ ❧ ❧ ❧

A MAN IS NOT OLD until regrets take the place of dreams.

John Barrymore

❧ ❧ ❧ ❧

THERE IS NOTHING SO POWERFUL as truth, and often nothing so strange.

Daniel Webster

❧ ❧ ❧ ❧

A MAN TRAVELS THE WORLD over in search of what he needs and returns home to find it.

George Moore

❧ ❧ ❧ ❧

IN PREPARING FOR BATTLE, I have always found that plans are useless, but planning is indispensable.

Dwight D. Eisenhower

❧ ❧ ❧ ❧

EVERY GENERATION REVOLTS against its fathers and makes friends with its grandfathers.

Lewis Mumford

❧ ❧ ❧ ❧

MAN IS LEAST HIMSELF when he talks in his own person. Give him a mask, and he will tell you the truth.

Oscar Wilde

❧ ❧ ❧ ❧

PERFECTION IS ACHIEVED, not when there is nothing more to add, but when there is nothing left to take away.

Antoine de Saint-Exupéry

❧ ❧ ❧ ❧

WHEN THE GOING GETS WEIRD, the weird turn pro.

Hunter S. Thompson

❧ ❧ ❧ ❧

WE CAN HELP MAKE the world safe for diversity. For, in the final analysis, our most basic common link is that we all inhabit this small planet. We all breathe the same air. We all cherish our children's future. And we are all mortal.

John F. Kennedy

❧ ❧ ❧ ❧

I TRY TO APPLY COLORS like words that shape poems, like notes that shape music.

Joan Miró

❧ ❧ ❧ ❧

LUCK is the residue of design.

Branch Rickey

❧ ❧ ❧ ❧

MAN PARTLY IS and wholly hopes to be.

Robert Browning

❧ ❧ ❧ ❧

BEAUTY WILL BE convulsive or will not be at all.

André Breton

❧ ❧ ❧ ❧

MAN IS THE ONLY kind of varmint who sets his own trap, baits it, then steps on it.

John Steinbeck

❧ ❧ ❧ ❧

NO MAN IS HAPPY without a delusion of some kind. Delusions are as necessary to our happiness as realities.

Christian Nestell Bovee

❧ ❧ ❧ ❧

YOU CAN CLOSE your eyes to reality but not to memories.

Stanislaw Jerzy Lec

❧ ❧ ❧ ❧

TREAT THE EARTH WELL: It was not given to you by your parents, it was loaned to you by your children. We do not inherit the earth from our ancestors; we borrow it from our children.

Native American proverb

❧ ❧ ❧ ❧

EVERYBODY IS IGNORANT, only on different subjects.

Will Rogers

❧ ❧ ❧ ❧

NO DIET WILL REMOVE all the fat from your body because the brain is entirely fat. Without a brain, you might look good, but all you could do is run for public office.

George Bernard Shaw

❧ ❧ ❧ ❧

MEN ARE BORN IGNORANT, not stupid; they are made stupid by education.

Bertrand Russell

❧ ❧ ❧ ❧

NEVER SPEND your money before you have it.

Thomas Jefferson

❧ ❧ ❧ ❧

WHY DO THEY CALL IT "rush hour," when nothing moves?

Robin Williams

❧ ❧ ❧ ❧

A PHOTOGRAPH IS A SECRET about a secret. The more it tells you the less you know.

Diane Arbus

❧ ❧ ❧ ❧

BUT ARE NOT THE DREAMS of poets and the tales of travelers notoriously false?

H. P. Lovecraft

❧ ❧ ❧ ❧

NOT EVERYTHING THAT CAN be counted counts, and not everything that counts can be counted.

Albert Einstein

❧ ❧ ❧ ❧

TO BE CONSCIOUS THAT YOU are ignorant is a great step to knowledge.

Benjamin Disraeli

❧ ❧ ❧ ❧

WHEN YOU REREAD A CLASSIC you do not see more in the book than you did before; you see more in you than there was before.

Clifton Fadiman

❧ ❧ ❧ ❧

THE WEAK HAVE ONE WEAPON: the errors of those who think they are strong.

Georges Bidault

❧ ❧ ❧ ❧

THE DRAWING SHOWS me at a glance what would be spread over ten pages in a book.

Ivan Turgenev

❧ ❧ ❧ ❧

I BELIEVE THAT IF ONE always looked at the skies, one would end up with wings.

Gustave Flaubert

❧ ❧ ❧ ❧

EVERYTHING WILL BE forgotten and nothing will be redressed.

Milan Kundera

❧ ❧ ❧ ❧

THE MAJOR DIFFERENCE between a thing that might go wrong and a thing that cannot possibly go wrong is that when a thing that cannot possibly go wrong goes wrong it usually turns out to be impossible to get at or repair.

Douglas Adams

❧ ❧ ❧ ❧

LIFE IS A GREAT BIG CANVAS, and you should throw all the paint on it you can.

Danny Kaye

❧ ❧ ❧ ❧

MAN MAKES HOLY what he believes, as he makes beautiful what he loves.

Ernest Renan

❧ ❧ ❧ ❧

A SMILE IS THE CHOSEN vehicle for all ambiguities.

Herman Melville

❧ ❧ ❧ ❧

LIFE IS A LONG lesson in humility.

James M. Barrie

❧ ❧ ❧ ❧

EDUCATION IS LEARNING what you didn't even know you didn't know.

Daniel J. Boorstin

❧ ❧ ❧ ❧

NONE OF US ARE RESPONSIBLE for our birth. Our responsibility is the use we make of life.

Joshua Henry Jones

❧ ❧ ❧ ❧

THE QUESTION OF WHETHER Machines Can Think is about as relevant as the question of whether Submarines Can Swim.

Edsger Dijkstra

❧ ❧ ❧ ❧

PEOPLE SAY that life is the thing, but I prefer reading.

Logan Pearsall Smith

❧ ❧ ❧ ❧

THE WORST PART of success is trying to find someone who is happy for you.

Bette Midler

❧ ❧ ❧ ❧

WHEN WE ARE UNABLE to find tranquility within ourselves, it is useless to seek it elsewhere.

François de La Rochefoucauld

❧ ❧ ❧ ❧

ONE ALWAYS BEGINS to forgive a place as soon as it's left behind.

Charles Dickens

❧ ❧ ❧ ❧

THE NEED TO BE RIGHT all the time is the biggest bar to new ideas. It is better to have enough ideas for some of them to be wrong than to be always right by having no ideas at all.

Edward de Bono

❧ ❧ ❧ ❧

IDEALISM INCREASES in direct proportion to one's distance from the problem.

John Galsworthy

❧ ❧ ❧ ❧

SOMETIMES IT IS MORE important to discover what one cannot do, than what one can do.

Lin Yutang

❧ ❧ ❧ ❧

AN EXPERT IS ONE who knows more and more about less and less.

Nicholas Murray Butler

❧ ❧ ❧ ❧

LIFE IS ONE long struggle in the dark.

Lucretius

❧ ❧ ❧ ❧

IT'S ALL RIGHT letting yourself go, as long as you can get yourself back.

Mick Jagger

❧ ❧ ❧ ❧

THE ONE THING that doesn't abide by majority rule is a person's conscience.

Harper Lee

❧ ❧ ❧ ❧

HUMOR IS A RUBBER SWORD—it allows you to make a point without drawing blood.

Mary Hirsch

❧ ❧ ❧ ❧

AS SOON AS YOU have made a thought, laugh at it.

Lao Tzu

❧ ❧ ❧ ❧

EACH MORNING SEES some task begin,
Each evening sees it close;
Something attempted, something done,
Has earned a night's repose.

Henry Wadsworth Longfellow

❧ ❧ ❧ ❧

SKIN IS A COVERING for our immortality.

Ever Garrison

❧ ❧ ❧ ❧

NO POWER IN SOCIETY, no hardship in your condition can depress you, keep you down, in knowledge, power, virtue, influence, but by your own consent.

William Ellery Channing

❧ ❧ ❧ ❧

BETTER TO FIGHT for something than live for nothing.

George S. Patton

❧ ❧ ❧ ❧

PROSPERITY IS ONLY an instrument to be used, not a deity to be worshipped.

Calvin Coolidge

❧ ❧ ❧ ❧

MISTAKES ARE ALMOST always of a sacred nature. Never try to correct them. On the contrary: rationalize them, understand them thoroughly. After that, it will be possible for you to sublimate them.

Salvador Dalí

❧ ❧ ❧ ❧

TRUTH IS AS IMPOSSIBLE to be soiled by any outward touch as the sunbeam.

John Milton

❧ ❧ ❧ ❧

THEY THAT GOVERN MOST, make least noise.

John Selden

❧ ❧ ❧ ❧

NEVER STAND BEGGING for that which you have the power to take.

Miguel de Cervantes

❖ ❖ ❖ ❖

I DO NOT WANT PEOPLE to be very agreeable, as it saves me the trouble of liking them a great deal.

Jane Austen

❖ ❖ ❖ ❖

WHO IS MORE FOOLISH, the child afraid of the dark or the man afraid of the light?

Maurice Freehill

❖ ❖ ❖ ❖

YOU CAN'T EXPECT a boy to be depraved until he has been to a good school.

Saki

❖ ❖ ❖ ❖

EVERY ARTIST makes himself born. It is very much harder than the other time, and longer.

Willa Cather

❖ ❖ ❖ ❖

YOU NEVER KNOW when you're making a memory.

Rickie Lee Jones

❖ ❖ ❖ ❖

THERE NEVER WAS a good War, or a bad Peace.

Benjamin Franklin

❧ ❧ ❧ ❧

THE PEOPLE WHO THINK they are happy should rummage through their dreams.

Edward Dahlberg

❧ ❧ ❧ ❧

WE ARE BORN to make manifest the glory of God that is within us. It is not just in some of us; it's in everyone.

Nelson Mandela

❧ ❧ ❧ ❧

LIVE YOUR QUESTIONS NOW, and perhaps even without knowing it, you will live along some distant day into your answers.

Rainer Maria Rilke

❧ ❧ ❧ ❧

HUMOR IS THE FIRST of the gifts to perish in a foreign tongue.

Virginia Woolf

❧ ❧ ❧ ❧

TELL ME, what is it you plan to do with your one wild and precious life?

Mary Oliver

❧ ❧ ❧ ❧

AND THOSE WHO were seen dancing were thought to be insane by those who could not hear the music.

Friedrich Nietzsche

⚜ ⚜ ⚜ ⚜

I HAVE GIVEN UP READING BOOKS; I find it takes my mind off myself.

Oscar Levant

⚜ ⚜ ⚜ ⚜

DOWN THESE MEAN STREETS a man must go who is not himself mean, who is neither tarnished nor afraid.

Raymond Chandler

⚜ ⚜ ⚜ ⚜

THERE COULD BE NO HONOR in a sure success, but much might be wrested from a sure defeat.

T. E. Lawrence

⚜ ⚜ ⚜ ⚜

DIFFICULTY IS THE EXCUSE that history never accepts.

Edward R. Murrow

⚜ ⚜ ⚜ ⚜

CLOTHES MAKE THE MAN, but nakedness makes the human being.

Kevin Kearney

⚜ ⚜ ⚜ ⚜

WEALTH IS LIKE SEAWATER—the more we drink, the thirstier we become, and the same is true of fame.

Arthur Schopenhauer

❧ ❧ ❧ ❧

I DON'T LIKE BELONGING to another person's dream.

Lewis Carroll

❧ ❧ ❧ ❧

LIBERTY EXISTS in proportion to wholesome restraint.

Daniel Webster

❧ ❧ ❧ ❧

POLITICS IS THE GENTLE ART of getting votes from the poor and campaign funds from the rich by promising to protect each from the other.

Oscar Ameringer

❧ ❧ ❧ ❧

OUR EXISTENCE is but a brief crack of light between two eternities of darkness.

Vladimir Nabokov

❧ ❧ ❧ ❧

YOU DON'T STOP LAUGHING because you grow old; you grow old because you stop laughing.

Michael Pritchard

❧ ❧ ❧ ❧

LIFE'S MOST URGENT QUESTION IS, what are you doing for others?

Dr. Martin Luther King, Jr.

⚜ ⚜ ⚜ ⚜

WORK EXPANDS so as to fill the time available for its completion.

C. Northcote Parkinson

⚜ ⚜ ⚜ ⚜

YOUR VISION WILL BECOME CLEAR only when you can look into your own heart. Who looks outside, dreams. Who looks inside, awakes.

Carl Jung

⚜ ⚜ ⚜ ⚜

YOU CANNOT SHAKE HANDS with a clenched fist.

Indira Gandhi

⚜ ⚜ ⚜ ⚜

THE VERY PURPOSE of existence is to reconcile the glowing opinion we have of ourselves with the appalling things that other people think about us.

Quentin Crisp

⚜ ⚜ ⚜ ⚜

CAPITALISM WITHOUT BANKRUPTCY is like Christianity without hell.

Frank Borman

⚜ ⚜ ⚜ ⚜

FAME IS A VAPOR; popularity an accident; the only earthly certainty is oblivion.

Mark Twain

❧ ❧ ❧ ❧

IT'S A FUNNY THING about life; if you refuse to accept anything but the best, you very often get it.

W. Somerset Maugham

❧ ❧ ❧ ❧

A PESSIMIST IS A PERSON who has had to listen to too many optimists.

Don Marquis

❧ ❧ ❧ ❧

SMALL ACTS, when multiplied by millions of people, can transform the world.

Howard Zinn

❧ ❧ ❧ ❧

IT IS A MARK OF MANY famous people that they cannot part with their brightest hour.

Lillian Hellman

❧ ❧ ❧ ❧

ONLY A FREE SOCIETY... can produce the technology that makes tyranny possible.

John Keith Laumer

❧ ❧ ❧ ❧

YOU WILL NEVER LIVE if you are looking for the meaning of life.

Albert Camus

❦ ❦ ❦ ❦

BETTER THAN A THOUSAND hollow words is one word that brings peace.

Buddha

❦ ❦ ❦ ❦

OH LONGING FOR places that were not
Cherished enough in that fleeting hour
How I long to make good from afar
The forgotten gesture, the additional act.

Rainer Maria Rilke

❦ ❦ ❦ ❦

THE DISTANCE IS NOTHING; it is only the first step that is difficult.

Marie du Deffand

❦ ❦ ❦ ❦

REALITY IS THAT STUFF WHICH, no matter what you believe, just won't go away.

David Paktor

❦ ❦ ❦ ❦

LIFE CONSISTS NOT in holding good cards but in playing those you hold well.

Josh Billings

❦ ❦ ❦ ❦

ADVICE IS WHAT we ask for when we already know the answer but wish we didn't.

Erica Jong

❧ ❧ ❧ ❧

"MY COUNTRY, RIGHT OR WRONG," is a thing that no patriot would think of saying except in a desperate case. It is like saying, "My mother, drunk or sober."

G. K. Chesterton

❧ ❧ ❧ ❧

WHY WE ARE HERE is an impenetrable question.

Edward Albee

❧ ❧ ❧ ❧

ONLY TWO THINGS ARE INFINITE: the universe and human stupidity, and I'm not sure about the former.

Albert Einstein

❧ ❧ ❧ ❧

WHERE OBSERVATION is concerned, chance favors only the prepared mind.

Louis Pasteur

❧ ❧ ❧ ❧

BLAMING MOTHER is just a negative way of clinging to her still.

Nancy Friday

❧ ❧ ❧ ❧

NOSTALGIA isn't what it used to be.

Peter De Vries

❧ ❧ ❧ ❧

IF YOU DON'T HAVE CONFIDENCE, you'll always find a way not to win.

Carl Lewis

❧ ❧ ❧ ❧

WHEN GREAT CHANGES occur in history, when great principles are involved, as a rule the majority are wrong. The minority are right.

Eugene V. Debs

❧ ❧ ❧ ❧

THE MORE THINGS CHANGE, the more they remain the same.

Alphonse Karr

❧ ❧ ❧ ❧

IT TAKES YOUR ENEMY and your friend, working together, to hurt you to the heart; the one to slander you and the other to get the news to you.

Mark Twain

❧ ❧ ❧ ❧

THERE SHOULD BE a solemn pause before we rush to judgment.

Thomas Erskine

❧ ❧ ❧ ❧

SPEECHES MEASURED by the hour, die with the hour.

Thomas Jefferson

🙵 🙵 🙵 🙵

IF WE DON'T CHANGE, we don't grow. If we don't grow, we are not really living.

Gail Sheehy

🙵 🙵 🙵 🙵

THE ONLY THING that's been a worse flop than the organization of nonviolence has been the organization of violence.

Joan Baez

🙵 🙵 🙵 🙵

WE ARE HERE TO ADD what we can to life, not to get what we can from life.

William Osler

🙵 🙵 🙵 🙵

A DWARF STANDING on the shoulders of a giant may see farther than a giant himself.

Robert Burton

🙵 🙵 🙵 🙵

THE GREATEST GLORY in living lies not in never falling, but in rising every time we fall.

Nelson Mandela

🙵 🙵 🙵 🙵

THE RATIO OF LITERACY to illiteracy is constant, but nowadays the illiterates can read and write.

Alberto Moravia

❧ ❧ ❧ ❧

A STATESMAN IS A POLITICIAN who's been dead 10 or 15 years.

Harry S. Truman

❧ ❧ ❧ ❧

THE LONGER ONE SAVES something before throwing it away, the sooner it will be needed after it is thrown away.

James J. Caufield

❧ ❧ ❧ ❧

IF YOU AREN'T CONFUSED by quantum physics, then you haven't really understood it.

Niels Bohr

❧ ❧ ❧ ❧

HOW DO WE KNOW when irrational exuberance has unduly escalated asset values?

Alan Greenspan

❧ ❧ ❧ ❧

YOU CAN'T WAIT FOR INSPIRATION. You have to go after it with a club.

Jack London

❧ ❧ ❧ ❧

THERE ARE ONLY two or three human stories, and they go on repeating themselves as fiercely as if they had never happened before.

Willa Cather

❖ ❖ ❖ ❖

ONLY THE PERSON who has faith in himself is able to be faithful to others.

Erich Fromm

❖ ❖ ❖ ❖

IT'S BETTER TO WRITE about things you feel than things that you know about.

L. P. Hartley

❖ ❖ ❖ ❖

A MAN MAY BUILD himself a throne of bayonets, but he cannot sit on it.

William Ralph Inge

❖ ❖ ❖ ❖

GOD ENTERS BY a private door into every individual.

Ralph Waldo Emerson

❖ ❖ ❖ ❖

WIT OUGHT TO BE a glorious treat, like caviar. Never spread it about like marmalade.

Noel Coward

❖ ❖ ❖ ❖

I AM A DEEPLY superficial person.

Andy Warhol

✤ ✤ ✤ ✤

PEOPLE TRAVEL for the same reason as they collect works of art: because the best people do it.

Aldous Huxley

✤ ✤ ✤ ✤

IF YOU DON'T GO to other men's funerals, they won't go to yours.

Clarence S. Day

✤ ✤ ✤ ✤

LIFE DOES NOT CONSIST in thinking, it consists in acting.

Woodrow Wilson

✤ ✤ ✤ ✤

IT'S LUCKY HAPPENSTANCE that women's liberation came along just when it did so that women can participate in the world arena and rescue the planet. Just in the nick of time.

Gretchen Cryer

✤ ✤ ✤ ✤

ABILITY MAY GET you to the top, but it takes character to keep you there.

John Wooden

✤ ✤ ✤ ✤

FOR SMALL CREATURES such as we, the vastness is bearable only through love.

Carl Sagan

❧ ❧ ❧ ❧

THE BIGGEST THINGS are always the easiest to do because there is no competition.

William Van Horne

❧ ❧ ❧ ❧

THE AIM OF LIFE is self-development. To realize one's nature perfectly—that is what each of us is here for.

Oscar Wilde

❧ ❧ ❧ ❧

TELEVISION HAS PROVED that people will look at anything rather than each other.

Ann Landers

❧ ❧ ❧ ❧

A MEMORANDUM IS WRITTEN not to inform the reader but to protect the writer.

Dean Acheson

❧ ❧ ❧ ❧

NOT EVEN COMPUTERS will replace committees, because committees buy computers.

Edward Shepherd Mead

❧ ❧ ❧ ❧

A GOOD LISTENER is not only popular everywhere, but after a while he knows something.

Wilson Mizner

❧ ❧ ❧ ❧

WHEN A TRUE GENIUS appears in the world you may know him by this sign: that all the dunces are in confederacy against him.

Jonathan Swift

❧ ❧ ❧ ❧

THE ARTIST IS NOTHING without the gift, but the gift is nothing without work.

Émile Zola

❧ ❧ ❧ ❧

YOU CAN SAFELY ASSUME that you've created God in your own image when it turns out that God hates all the same people you do.

Anne Lamott

❧ ❧ ❧ ❧

THIS WORLD IS A COMEDY to those who think, a tragedy to those who feel.

Horace Walpole

❧ ❧ ❧ ❧

WE ARE THE CURATORS of life on earth; we hold it in the palm of our hand.

Dr. Helen Caldicott

❧ ❧ ❧ ❧

IF I WERE TWO-FACED, would I be wearing this one?

Abraham Lincoln

❧ ❧ ❧ ❧

A NEW SCIENTIFIC TRUTH does not triumph by convincing its opponents and making them see the light, but rather because its opponents eventually die, and a new generation grows up that is familiar with it.

Max Planck

❧ ❧ ❧ ❧

I AM PATIENT WITH STUPIDITY but not with those who are proud of it.

Edith Sitwell

❧ ❧ ❧ ❧

NOTHING FIXES A THING so intensely in the memory as the wish to forget it.

Michel de Montaigne

❧ ❧ ❧ ❧

IT'S EASY TO MAKE A BUCK. It's a lot tougher to make a difference.

Tom Brokaw

❧ ❧ ❧ ❧

WARS HAVE NEVER HURT anybody except the people who die.

Salvador Dalí

❧ ❧ ❧ ❧

I PAINT SELF-PORTRAITS because I am so often alone, because I am the person I know best.

Frida Kahlo

❖ ❖ ❖ ❖

AN ARTIST'S ONLY CONCERN is to shoot for some kind of perfection, and on his own terms, not anyone else's.

J. D. Salinger

❖ ❖ ❖ ❖

YOU CANNOT FIGHT against the future. Time is on our side.

William E. Gladstone

❖ ❖ ❖ ❖

TAKE SIDES. NEUTRALITY helps the oppressor, never the victim. Silence encourages the tormentor, never the tormented.

Elie Wiesel

❖ ❖ ❖ ❖

ALL HUMAN SOCIETIES go through fads in which they temporarily either adopt practices of little use or else abandon practices of considerable use.

Jared Diamond

❖ ❖ ❖ ❖

THE BIGGER THEY ARE, the further they have to fall.

Robert Fitzsimmons

❖ ❖ ❖ ❖

TO PUT MEANING in one's life may end in madness, but life without meaning is the torture of restlessness and vague desire—It is a boat longing for the sea and yet afraid.

Edgar Lee Masters

❧ ❧ ❧ ❧

THERE IS NO WAY to peace. Peace is the way.

A. J. Muste

❧ ❧ ❧ ❧

IF WE MAKE PEACEFUL revolution impossible, we make violent revolution inevitable.

John F. Kennedy

❧ ❧ ❧ ❧

YOU'RE EITHER PART of the solution or you're part of the problem.

Eldridge Cleaver

❧ ❧ ❧ ❧

THE TRAGEDY OF LIFE is not that man loses, but that he almost wins.

Heywood Broun

❧ ❧ ❧ ❧

WHAT GOOD WILL IT BE for a man if he gains the whole world, yet forfeits his soul?

Matthew 16:26 (NIV)

❧ ❧ ❧ ❧

OLD AGE IS THE MOST unexpected of all the things that happen to a man.

Leon Trotsky

❧ ❧ ❧ ❧

WE MUST NOT ALWAYS talk in the marketplace of what happens to us in the forest.

Nathaniel Hawthorne

❧ ❧ ❧ ❧

THE ONLY FENCE against the world is a thorough knowledge of it.

John Locke

❧ ❧ ❧ ❧

ONE OF THE SIGNS of passing youth is the birth of a sense of fellowship with other human beings as we take our place among them.

Virginia Woolf

❧ ❧ ❧ ❧

WE ARE THE ONLY KIND of company whose assets all walk out of the gate at night.

Louis B. Mayer

❧ ❧ ❧ ❧

MOST MEN EMPLOY the first years of their life in making the last miserable.

Jean de La Bruyère

❧ ❧ ❧ ❧

MY PHILOSOPHY IS that not only are you responsible for your life, but doing the best at this moment puts you in the best place for the next moment.

Oprah Winfrey

❖ ❖ ❖ ❖

HATRED IS THE COWARD'S revenge for being intimidated.

George Bernard Shaw

❖ ❖ ❖ ❖

IN OUR FAMILY, there was no clear line between religion and fly-fishing.

Norman Maclean

❖ ❖ ❖ ❖

LOVE IS AN ACT of endless forgiveness, a tender look which becomes a habit.

Peter Ustinov

❖ ❖ ❖ ❖

I CAN'T SAY AS EVER I was lost, but I was bewildered once for three days.

Daniel Boone

❖ ❖ ❖ ❖

LIFE, AS IT IS CALLED, is for most of us one long postponement.

Henry Miller

❖ ❖ ❖ ❖

A FRIEND WILL HELP YOU MOVE. A best friend will help you move...the body.

Dave Attell

❧ ❧ ❧ ❧

IF WORK WAS A GOOD THING the rich would have it all and not let you do it.

Elmore Leonard

❧ ❧ ❧ ❧

THE BEST, MOST BEAUTIFUL things in the world cannot be seen, or even touched. They must be felt with the heart.

Helen Keller

❧ ❧ ❧ ❧

FIRST SAY TO YOURSELF what you would be; and then do what you have to do.

Epictetus

❧ ❧ ❧ ❧

IF YOU ESCAPE FROM PEOPLE too often, you wind up escaping from yourself.

Marvin Gaye

❧ ❧ ❧ ❧

FATE IS BEING KIND TO ME. Fate doesn't want me to be famous too young.

Duke Ellington

❧ ❧ ❧ ❧

A SAD SOUL WILL KILL you quicker, far quicker, than a germ.

John Steinbeck

❖ ❖ ❖ ❖

HISTORY IS BUT PAST POLITICS, and politics are but present history.

Edward Augustus Freeman

❖ ❖ ❖ ❖

FORTUNATELY PSYCHOANALYSIS is not the only way to resolve inner conflicts. Life itself still remains a very effective therapist.

Karen Horney

❖ ❖ ❖ ❖

THE BEST WAY TO find out if you can trust somebody is to trust them.

Ernest Hemingway

❖ ❖ ❖ ❖

IF WE WAIT FOR THE MOMENT when everything, absolutely everything is ready, we shall never begin.

Ivan Turgenev

❖ ❖ ❖ ❖

IT DOES NOT DO to dwell on dreams and forget to live, remember that.

J. K. Rowling

❖ ❖ ❖ ❖

WE'RE FOOLS WHETHER we dance or not, so we might as well dance.

Anonymous

❖ ❖ ❖ ❖

PRINCIPLES HAVE NO real force except when one is well fed.

Mark Twain

❖ ❖ ❖ ❖

THERE WAS NO RESPECT for youth when I was young, and now that I am old, there is no respect for age—I missed it coming and going.

J. B. Priestley

❖ ❖ ❖ ❖

OF ALL FEATS OF SKILL, the most difficult is that of being honest.

Comtesse Diane (Marie de Beausacq)

❖ ❖ ❖ ❖

REMEMBER, PEOPLE WILL JUDGE you by your actions, not your intentions. You may have a heart of gold—but so does a hard-boiled egg.

Anonymous

❖ ❖ ❖ ❖

WE HAVE TO DISTRUST each other. It is our only defense against betrayal.

Tennessee Williams

❖ ❖ ❖ ❖

BUT MAN IS NOT MADE FOR DEFEAT. A man can be destroyed but not defeated.

Ernest Hemingway

❧ ❧ ❧ ❧

ONE OF THE SYMPTOMS of an approaching nervous breakdown is the belief that one's work is terribly important.

Bertrand Russell

❧ ❧ ❧ ❧

ONLY TWO CLASSES of books are of universal appeal: the very best and the very worst.

Ford Madox Ford

❧ ❧ ❧ ❧

HISTORY NEVER LOOKS like history when you are living through it. It always looks confusing and messy, and it always feels uncomfortable.

John W. Gardner

❧ ❧ ❧ ❧

ONE OF THE KEYS to happiness is a real bad memory.

Rita Mae Brown

❧ ❧ ❧ ❧

YOU CANNOT HAVE EVERYTHING. I mean, where would you put it?

Steven Wright

❧ ❧ ❧ ❧

YE SHALL KNOW THE TRUTH, and the truth shall make
you mad.

Aldous Huxley

🙰 🙰 🙰 🙰

TIME IS A GREAT LEGALIZER, even in the field of morals.

H. L. Mencken

🙰 🙰 🙰 🙰

A MAN IS A CRITIC when he cannot be an artist, in the same
way that a man becomes an informer when he cannot be a
soldier.

Gustave Flaubert

🙰 🙰 🙰 🙰

INSANITY: a perfectly rational adjustment to the insane world.

R. D. Laing

🙰 🙰 🙰 🙰

BEAUTIFUL YOUNG PEOPLE are accidents of nature, but beautiful
old people are works of art.

Eleanor Roosevelt

🙰 🙰 🙰 🙰

THAT'S OUR MOTTO. We want freedom by any means necessary.
We want justice by any means necessary. We want equality by
any means necessary.

Malcolm X

🙰 🙰 🙰 🙰

THE SECRET TO LIFE: replace one worry with another.

Charles Schulz

✣ ✣ ✣ ✣

DANCING IS THE LOFTIEST, the most moving, the most beautiful of the arts, because it is no mere translation or abstraction from life; it is life itself.

Havelock Ellis

✣ ✣ ✣ ✣

FORGIVENESS IS NOT an occasional act; it is a permanent attitude.

Dr. Martin Luther King, Jr.

✣ ✣ ✣ ✣

ALL, EVERYTHING THAT I UNDERSTAND, I understand only because I love.

Leo Tolstoy

✣ ✣ ✣ ✣

NEXT TO THE VERY YOUNG, I suppose the very old are the most selfish.

William Makepeace Thackeray

✣ ✣ ✣ ✣

MY HAPPINESS IS NOT the means to any end. It is the end. It is its own goal. It is its own purpose.

Ayn Rand

✣ ✣ ✣ ✣

CITY LIFE. Millions of people being lonesome together.

Henry David Thoreau

❧ ❧ ❧ ❧

TRUST MEN, and they will be true to you; treat them greatly, and they will show themselves great.

Ralph Waldo Emerson

❧ ❧ ❧ ❧

DO A COMMON THING in an uncommon manner.

Booker T. Washington

❧ ❧ ❧ ❧

MOST AFFECTIONS ARE HABITS or duties we lack the courage to end.

Henri de Montherlant

❧ ❧ ❧ ❧

THERE ARE TWO CLASSES of people in this world, those who sin, and those who are sinned against. If a man must belong to either, he had better belong to the first than to the second.

Samuel Butler

❧ ❧ ❧ ❧

TO LEARN SOMETHING new, take the path that you took yesterday.

John Burroughs

❧ ❧ ❧ ❧

IN LIFE, MANY THOUGHTS are born in the course of a moment, an hour, a day. Some are dreams, some visions. Often, we are unable to distinguish between them. To some, they are the same; however, not all dreams are visions. Much energy is lost in fanciful dreams that never bear fruit. But visions are messages from the Great Spirit, each for a different purpose in life. Consequently, one person's vision may not be that of another. To have a vision, one must be prepared to receive it, and when it comes, to accept it. Thus when these inner urges become reality, only then can visions be fulfilled. The spiritual side of life knows everyone's heart and who to trust. How could a vision ever be given to someone to harbor if that person could not be trusted to carry it out? The message is simple. Commitment precedes vision.

High Eagle

🙕 🙕 🙕 🙕

THE ACT OF WRITING is the act of discovering what you believe.

David Hare

🙕 🙕 🙕 🙕

OUT OF THE STRAIN of the Doing,
Into the peace of the Done.

Julia Louise Woodruff

🙕 🙕 🙕 🙕

THERE ARE THREE INGREDIENTS in the good life: learning, earning, and yearning.

Christopher Morley

🙕 🙕 🙕 🙕

MEMORY, OF ALL the powers of the mind, is the most delicate and frail.

Ben Jonson

❧ ❧ ❧ ❧

DOING WHAT'S RIGHT isn't the problem. It's knowing what's right.

Lyndon B. Johnson

❧ ❧ ❧ ❧

A COMPROMISE IS THE ART of dividing a cake in such a way that everyone believes that he has the biggest piece.

Ludwig Erhard

❧ ❧ ❧ ❧

IT IS NOT NECESSARY to understand things in order to argue about them.

Pierre-Augustin Caron de Beaumarchais

❧ ❧ ❧ ❧

KNOWLEDGE IS THE CONFORMITY of the object and the intellect.

Averroës

❧ ❧ ❧ ❧

WE HAVE NO MORE RIGHT to consume happiness without producing it than to consume wealth without producing it.

George Bernard Shaw

❧ ❧ ❧ ❧

DON'T THINK THERE are no crocodiles because the water is calm.

Anonymous

❧ ❧ ❧ ❧

REALITY IS A CRUTCH for people who can't cope with drugs.

Jane Wagner

❧ ❧ ❧ ❧

THE GREAT TRAGEDY of science—the slaying of a beautiful hypothesis by an ugly fact.

Thomas Henry Huxley

❧ ❧ ❧ ❧

YOU'RE ONLY HERE for a short visit. Don't hurry. Don't worry. And be sure to smell the flowers along the way.

Walter Hagen

❧ ❧ ❧ ❧

STILL 'ROUND THE CORNER there may wait,
A new road or a secret gate.

J.R.R. Tolkien

❧ ❧ ❧ ❧

IF IT WEREN'T FOR THE FACT that the TV set and the refrigerator are so far apart, some of us wouldn't get any exercise at all.

Joey Adams

❧ ❧ ❧ ❧

AS LONG AS YOU'RE GOING to be thinking anyway, think big.

Donald Trump

❖ ❖ ❖ ❖

IMAGINE WHAT A HARMONIOUS world it could be if every single person, both young and old, shared a little of what he is good at doing.

Quincy Jones

❖ ❖ ❖ ❖

WE CAN DO ANYTHING we want to do if we stick to it long enough.

Helen Keller

❖ ❖ ❖ ❖

SUPERSTITION is the religion of feeble minds.

Edmund Burke

❖ ❖ ❖ ❖

AS MANY PEOPLE DIE from an excess of timidity as from bravery.

Norman Mailer

❖ ❖ ❖ ❖

THE BIG SECRET IN LIFE is that there is no big secret. Whatever your goal, you can get there if you're willing to work.

Oprah Winfrey

❖ ❖ ❖ ❖

CAN ONE BE A SAINT without God? That's the problem, in fact the only problem, I'm up against today.

Albert Camus

❧ ❧ ❧ ❧

ADVICE IS SELDOM WELCOME, and those who want it the most always like it the least.

Philip Dormer Stanhope (Lord Chesterfield)

❧ ❧ ❧ ❧

IF TOAST ALWAYS LANDS butter-side down, and cats always land on their feet, what happens if you strap toast on the back of a cat and drop it?

Steven Wright

❧ ❧ ❧ ❧

A MAN DOES WHAT HE MUST—in spite of personal consequences, in spite of obstacles and dangers and pressures, and that is the basis of all human morality.

John F. Kennedy

❧ ❧ ❧ ❧

YOU SHALL LOVE your neighbor as yourself.

Leviticus 19:18 (KJV)

❧ ❧ ❧ ❧

WISDOM CONSISTS of the anticipation of consequences.

Norman Cousins

❧ ❧ ❧ ❧

EXISTENTIALISM MEANS that no one else can take a bath for you.

Delmore Schwartz

❖ ❖ ❖ ❖

I DON'T KNOW WHY it is we are in such a hurry to get up when we fall down. You might think we would lie there and rest a while.

Max Eastman

❖ ❖ ❖ ❖

THERE IS MUCH PLEASURE to be gained from useless knowledge.

Bertrand Russell

❖ ❖ ❖ ❖

THE GREAT ADVANTAGE of living in a large family is that early lesson of life's essential unfairness.

Nancy Mitford

❖ ❖ ❖ ❖

WHAT SMALL POTATOES we all are, compared with what we might be!

Charles Dudley Warner

❖ ❖ ❖ ❖

WE DIE. That may be the meaning of life. But we do language. That may be the measure of our lives.

Toni Morrison

❖ ❖ ❖ ❖

MEN ARE MORE APT to be mistaken in their generalizations than in their particular observations.

Niccolò Machiavelli

❀ ❀ ❀ ❀

DELAY IS THE DEADLIEST form of denial.

C. Northcote Parkinson

❀ ❀ ❀ ❀

PAINTING IS A BLIND MAN'S profession. He paints not what he sees, but what he feels, what he tells himself about what he has seen.

Pablo Picasso

❀ ❀ ❀ ❀

A CRITIC IS A PERSON who knows the way but can't drive the car.

Kenneth Tynan

❀ ❀ ❀ ❀

I HOPE YOU HAVE not been leading a double life, pretending to be wicked and being really good all the time. That would be hypocrisy.

Oscar Wilde

❀ ❀ ❀ ❀

A MATHEMATICIAN IS A MACHINE for turning coffee into theorems.

Paul Erdos

❀ ❀ ❀ ❀

STRENGTH DOES NOT come from winning. Your struggles develop your strengths. When you go through hardships and decide not to surrender, that is strength.

Arnold Schwarzenegger

❧ ❧ ❧ ❧

HOW WONDERFUL IT IS that nobody need wait a single moment before starting to improve the world.

Anne Frank

❧ ❧ ❧ ❧

PEOPLE NEED A LEADER more than a leader needs people.

Bob Dylan

❧ ❧ ❧ ❧

THE HISTORY OF IDEAS is the history of the grudges of solitary men.

E. M. Cioran

❧ ❧ ❧ ❧

NOBODY DIES from lack of sex. It is lack of love we die from.

Margaret Atwood

❧ ❧ ❧ ❧

NEARLY ALL MEN DIE of their remedies, and not of their illnesses.

Jean-Baptiste Poquelin Molière

❧ ❧ ❧ ❧

PAIN IS TEMPORARY. It may last a minute, or an hour, or a day, or a year, but eventually it will subside and something else will take its place. If I quit, however, it lasts forever.

Lance Armstrong

❧ ❧ ❧ ❧

EVERYONE WHO RECEIVES the protection of society owes a return for the benefit.

John Stuart Mill

❧ ❧ ❧ ❧

MEETINGS ARE INDISPENSABLE when you don't want to do anything.

John Kenneth Galbraith

❧ ❧ ❧ ❧

THE GREAT MAN is the one who does not lose his child's heart.

Mencius

❧ ❧ ❧ ❧

CLIMATE IS WHAT you expect, weather is what you get.

Robert A. Heinlein

❧ ❧ ❧ ❧

AMBITION IF IT FEEDS AT ALL, does so on the ambition of others.

Susan Sontag

❧ ❧ ❧ ❧

PEOPLE WILL DO ANYTHING, no matter how absurd, in order to avoid facing their own souls.

Carl Jung

❧ ❧ ❧ ❧

DON'T PAY ANY ATTENTION to what they write about you. Just measure it in inches.

Andy Warhol

❧ ❧ ❧ ❧

SELL A COUNTRY! Why not sell the air, the clouds, and the great sea, as well as the earth? Did not the Great Spirit make them all for the use of his children?

Tecumseh

❧ ❧ ❧ ❧

THE TROUBLE WITH being poor is that it takes up all your time.

Willem de Kooning

❧ ❧ ❧ ❧

EXPERIENCE IS WHAT you get while looking for something else.

Federico Fellini

❧ ❧ ❧ ❧

A MAN HAD NEVER yet been hung for breaking the spirit of a law.

Grover Cleveland

❧ ❧ ❧ ❧

THE PUBLIC IS THE ONLY critic whose opinion is worth anything at all.

Mark Twain

⚜ ⚜ ⚜ ⚜

WHEN A MAN TELLS YOU that he got rich through hard work, ask him: "Whose?"

Don Marquis

⚜ ⚜ ⚜ ⚜

WE ARE NOT RETREATING—we are advancing in another direction.

General Douglas MacArthur

⚜ ⚜ ⚜ ⚜

A MINIMUM-WAGE LAW IS, in reality, a law that makes it illegal for an employer to hire a person with limited skills.

Milton Friedman

⚜ ⚜ ⚜ ⚜

EXCESS ON OCCASION IS exhilarating. It prevents moderation from acquiring the deadening effect of a habit.

W. Somerset Maugham

⚜ ⚜ ⚜ ⚜

BE ASHAMED TO DIE until you have won some victory for humanity.

Horace Mann

⚜ ⚜ ⚜ ⚜

ADVERTISEMENTS CONTAIN the only truths to be relied on in a newspaper.

Thomas Jefferson

⚜ ⚜ ⚜ ⚜

SOMETIMES IT'S NECESSARY to go a long distance out of the way in order to come back a short distance correctly.

Edward Albee

⚜ ⚜ ⚜ ⚜

IT IS THE WISDOM of crocodiles, that shed tears when they would devour.

Francis Bacon

⚜ ⚜ ⚜ ⚜

THERE ARE ONLY THREE THINGS to be done with a woman. You can love her, suffer for her, or turn her into literature.

Lawrence Durrell

⚜ ⚜ ⚜ ⚜

UNTIL THE DAY of his death, no man can be sure of his courage.

Jean Anouilh

⚜ ⚜ ⚜ ⚜

DON'T BE AFRAID to go out on a limb. That's where the fruit is.

H. Jackson Browne

⚜ ⚜ ⚜ ⚜

SURPLUS WEALTH IS A SACRED trust which its possessor is bound to administer in his lifetime for the good of the community.

Andrew Carnegie

❖ ❖ ❖ ❖

SANITY is a madness put to good uses.

George Santayana

❖ ❖ ❖ ❖

POETRY IS ABOUT as much a "criticism of life" as red-hot iron is a criticism of fire.

Ezra Pound

❖ ❖ ❖ ❖

IT IS MUCH MORE COMFORTABLE to be mad and know it, than to be sane and have one's doubts.

G. B. Burgin

❖ ❖ ❖ ❖

WHEN THE FACTS CHANGE, I change my mind. What do you do, sir?

John Maynard Keynes

❖ ❖ ❖ ❖

ALL MY LIFE, affection has been showered on me, and every forward step I have made has been taken in spite of it.

George Bernard Shaw

❖ ❖ ❖ ❖

AN ARTIST NEVER REALLY finishes his work; he merely abandons it.

Paul Valéry

❧ ❧ ❧ ❧

HATRED COMES FROM THE HEART; contempt from the head; and neither feeling is quite within our control.

Arthur Schopenhauer

❧ ❧ ❧ ❧

THE GREATEST OBSTACLE to discovery is not ignorance—it is the illusion of knowledge.

Daniel J. Boorstin

❧ ❧ ❧ ❧

EVERYBODY ON THIS PLANET is separated by only six other people. Six degrees of separation. Between us and everybody else on this planet.

John Guare

❧ ❧ ❧ ❧

LIFE IS A MODERATELY good play with a badly written third act.

Truman Capote

❧ ❧ ❧ ❧

NOBODY CARES IF YOU can't dance well. Just get up and dance.

Dave Barry

❧ ❧ ❧ ❧

THE LOVING are the daring.

Bayard Taylor

⚜ ⚜ ⚜ ⚜

SOLUTIONS are not the answer.

Richard Nixon

⚜ ⚜ ⚜ ⚜

IF MEN KNEW what women laughed about, they would never sleep with us.

Erica Jong

⚜ ⚜ ⚜ ⚜

IN SCIENCE ONE TRIES to tell people, in such a way as to be understood by everyone, something that no one ever knew before. But in poetry, it's the exact opposite.

Paul Dirac

⚜ ⚜ ⚜ ⚜

A BAD CAUSE WILL ever be supported by bad means and bad men.

Thomas Paine

⚜ ⚜ ⚜ ⚜

I THEREFORE CLAIM to show, not how men think in myths, but how myths operate in men's minds without their being aware of the fact.

Claude Lévi-Strauss

⚜ ⚜ ⚜ ⚜

SORROW IS TRANQUILITY remembered in emotion.

Dorothy Parker

❧ ❧ ❧ ❧

TO GENERALIZE IS TO BE AN IDIOT. To particularize is the alone distinction of merit—general knowledges are those knowledges that idiots possess.

William Blake

❧ ❧ ❧ ❧

LIFE IS DOUBT, and faith without doubt is nothing but death.

Miguel de Unamuno

❧ ❧ ❧ ❧

ANYONE WHO HAS NEVER made a mistake has never tried anything new.

Albert Einstein

❧ ❧ ❧ ❧

WHENEVER A FRIEND SUCCEEDS, a little something in me dies.

Gore Vidal

❧ ❧ ❧ ❧

AFTER A CERTAIN number of years, our faces become our biographies.

Cynthia Ozick

❧ ❧ ❧ ❧

ART WASHES AWAY from the soul the dust of everyday life.

Pablo Picasso

🔸 🔸 🔸 🔸

SYNERGY MEANS BEHAVIOR of whole systems unpredicted by the behavior of their parts.

Buckminster Fuller

🔸 🔸 🔸 🔸

A BELIEF IN A SUPERNATURAL source of evil is not necessary; men alone are quite capable of every wickedness.

Joseph Conrad

🔸 🔸 🔸 🔸

A CYNIC IS A MAN WHO, when he smells flowers, looks around for a coffin.

H. L. Mencken

🔸 🔸 🔸 🔸

A GREAT MAN DOES NOT lose his self-possession when he is afflicted; the ocean is not made muddy by the falling in of its banks.

Panchatantra

🔸 🔸 🔸 🔸

THERE NEVER WAS a democracy yet that did not commit suicide.

John Quincy Adams

🔸 🔸 🔸 🔸

IF YOU DESIRE TO TAKE from a thing, first you must give to it.

Lao Tzu

✿ ✿ ✿ ✿

I AM A HUMANIST, which means, in part, that I have tried to behave decently without any expectations of rewards or punishment after I'm dead.

Kurt Vonnegut

✿ ✿ ✿ ✿

THE WORLD BEGAN without man, and it will end without him.

Claude Lévi-Strauss

✿ ✿ ✿ ✿

UNLESS YOU CHOOSE to do great things with it, it makes no difference how much you are rewarded, or how much power you have.

Oprah Winfrey

✿ ✿ ✿ ✿

THE HIGHEST RESULT of education is tolerance.

Helen Keller

✿ ✿ ✿ ✿

THE ATTEMPT TO MAKE heaven on earth invariably produces hell.

Karl Popper

✿ ✿ ✿ ✿

ALWAYS GIVE A WORD or a sign of salute when meeting or passing a friend, even a stranger, when in a lonely place.

Tecumseh

✤ ✤ ✤ ✤

TAKE CALCULATED RISKS. That is quite different from being rash.

George S. Patton

✤ ✤ ✤ ✤

THE OBSCURE WE SEE EVENTUALLY. The completely apparent takes a little longer.

Edward R. Murrow

✤ ✤ ✤ ✤

THE ONLY REWARD of virtue is virtue; the only way to have a friend is to be one.

Ralph Waldo Emerson

✤ ✤ ✤ ✤

THE ONLY THING which makes one place more attractive to me than another is the quantity of heart I find in it.

Jane Welsh Carlyle

✤ ✤ ✤ ✤

I FIRST LEARNED the concepts of nonviolence in my marriage.

Mohandas Gandhi

✤ ✤ ✤ ✤

FAITH MAY BE DEFINED briefly as an illogical belief in the occurrence of the improbable.

H. L. Mencken

✤ ✤ ✤ ✤

WHEN I CAME HOME I expected a surprise and there was no surprise for me, so, of course, I was surprised.

Ludwig Wittgenstein

✤ ✤ ✤ ✤

NO ONE CAN MAKE YOU feel inferior without your consent.

Eleanor Roosevelt

✤ ✤ ✤ ✤

THE FREE THINKING of one age is the common sense of the next.

Matthew Arnold

✤ ✤ ✤ ✤

I CANNOT HELP IT that my paintings do not sell. The time will come when people will see that they are worth more than the price of the paint.

Vincent van Gogh

✤ ✤ ✤ ✤

THE OPTIMIST sees the donut
But the pessimist sees the hole.

McLandburgh Wilson

✤ ✤ ✤ ✤

ONE OF THE VIRTUES of being very young is that you don't let the facts get in the way of your imagination.

Sam Levenson

❧ ❧ ❧ ❧

HE HAD GROWN UP in a country run by politicians who sent the pilots to man the bombers to kill the babies to make the world safe for children to grow up in.

Ursula K. Le Guin

❧ ❧ ❧ ❧

ACTION . . . IS THE LAST RESOURCE of those who know not how to dream.

Oscar Wilde

❧ ❧ ❧ ❧

HUMAN SPEECH IS LIKE a cracked kettle on which we tap crude rhythms for bears to dance to, while we long to make music that will melt the stars.

Gustave Flaubert

❧ ❧ ❧ ❧

I HATE intolerant people.

Gloria Steinem

❧ ❧ ❧ ❧

POWER IS the great aphrodisiac.

Henry Kissinger

❧ ❧ ❧ ❧

THE MAIN THING about acting is honesty. If you can fake that, you've got it made.

George Burns

❧ ❧ ❧ ❧

HONOR FOLLOWS those who flee it.

Anonymous

❧ ❧ ❧ ❧

A WISE MAN HEARS one word and understands two.

Yiddish proverb

❧ ❧ ❧ ❧

ONE DOES NOT SELL the earth upon which the people walk.

Crazy Horse

❧ ❧ ❧ ❧

AND WE SHOULD CONSIDER every day lost on which we have not danced at least once. And we should call every truth false which was not accompanied by at least one laugh.

Friedrich Nietzsche

❧ ❧ ❧ ❧

IT IS FAR BETTER to grasp the Universe as it really is than to persist in delusion, however satisfying and reassuring.

Carl Sagan

❧ ❧ ❧ ❧

ALL THAT IS NECESSARY for the triumph of evil is that good men do nothing.

Edmund Burke

❖ ❖ ❖ ❖

A PAINTER PAINTS his pictures on canvas. But musicians paint their pictures on silence. We provide the music, and you provide the silence.

Leopold Stokowski

❖ ❖ ❖ ❖

THERE IS NOTHING HARDER than the softness of indifference.

Juan Montalvo

❖ ❖ ❖ ❖

THE HEALTHY MAN does not torture others—generally, it is the tortured who turn into torturers.

Carl Jung

❖ ❖ ❖ ❖

THE ONLY COMPLETELY consistent people are the dead.

Aldous Huxley

❖ ❖ ❖ ❖

WE WORK TO BECOME, not to acquire.

Elbert Hubbard

❖ ❖ ❖ ❖

DEMOCRACY IS NOT a state in which people act like sheep.

Mohandas Gandhi

❧ ❧ ❧ ❧

WHEN ONE DOOR CLOSES another door opens; but we often look so long and so regretfully upon the closed door that we do not see the one which has opened for us.

Alexander Graham Bell

❧ ❧ ❧ ❧

MARRIAGE HAS MANY PAINS, but celibacy has no pleasures.

Samuel Johnson

❧ ❧ ❧ ❧

PREDICTION IS VERY DIFFICULT, especially about the future.

Niels Bohr

❧ ❧ ❧ ❧

THROW YOUR DREAMS into space like a kite, and you do not know what it will bring back—a new life, a new friend, a new love, a new country.

Anaïs Nin

❧ ❧ ❧ ❧

MEN ARE NEARLY ALWAYS willing to believe what they wish.

Julius Caesar

❧ ❧ ❧ ❧

IT IS NOT IN LIFE but in art that self-fulfillment is to be found.

George Woodcock

✤ ✤ ✤ ✤

NEVER LIE IN BED at night asking yourself questions you can't answer.

Charles Schulz

✤ ✤ ✤ ✤

I WANT TO STAY as close to the edge as I can without going over. Out on the edge, you see all kinds of things you can't see from the center.

Kurt Vonnegut

✤ ✤ ✤ ✤

TURN YOUR FACE to the sun and the shadows fall behind you.

Maori proverb

✤ ✤ ✤ ✤

WHERE I WAS BORN and where and how I have lived is unimportant. It is what I have done with where I have been that should be of interest.

Georgia O'Keeffe

✤ ✤ ✤ ✤

EVEN A CLOCK that does not work is right twice a day.

Polish proverb

✤ ✤ ✤ ✤

A PROBLEM WELL STATED is a problem half solved.

Charles F. Kettering

⚜ ⚜ ⚜ ⚜

IF YOU WANT SOMETHING very, very badly, let it go free. If it comes back to you, it's yours forever. If it doesn't, it was never yours to begin with.

Jess Lair

⚜ ⚜ ⚜ ⚜

THE MOST MERCIFUL THING in the world, I think, is the inability of the human mind to correlate all its contents.

H. P. Lovecraft

⚜ ⚜ ⚜ ⚜

WE DRIVE INTO the future using only our rear view mirror.

Marshall McLuhan

⚜ ⚜ ⚜ ⚜

CONTENTMENT IS, after all, simply refined indolence.

Thomas C. Haliburton

⚜ ⚜ ⚜ ⚜

RATHER THAN CONTINUING to seek the truth, simply let go of your views.

Buddha

⚜ ⚜ ⚜ ⚜

WHATEVER IS WORTH DOING at all is worth doing well.

Philip Dormer Stanhope (Lord Chesterfield)

⚜ ⚜ ⚜ ⚜

MAN WAS MADE at the end of the week's work, when God was tired.

Mark Twain

⚜ ⚜ ⚜ ⚜

CHILDREN SHOW SCARS like medals. Lovers use them as secrets to reveal. A scar is what happens when the word is made flesh.

Leonard Cohen

⚜ ⚜ ⚜ ⚜

BLESSED ARE THE MEEK: for they shall inherit the earth.

Matthew 5:5 (KJV)

⚜ ⚜ ⚜ ⚜

A MAN WITHOUT FAITH is like a fish without a bicycle.

Charles S. Harris

⚜ ⚜ ⚜ ⚜

WHAT I'M TRYING to describe is that it's impossible to get out of your skin into somebody else's.... Somebody else's tragedy is not the same as your own.

Diane Arbus

⚜ ⚜ ⚜ ⚜

IT DOES NOT REQUIRE many words to speak the truth.

Chief Joseph

❧ ❧ ❧ ❧

INSANE PEOPLE ARE ALWAYS sure that they are fine. It's only the sane people who are willing to admit that they're crazy.

Nora Ephron

❧ ❧ ❧ ❧

THE TEST OF A REAL COMEDIAN is whether you laugh at him before he opens his mouth.

George Jean Nathan

❧ ❧ ❧ ❧

THE EDGE . . . There is no honest way to explain it because the only people who really know where it is are the ones who have gone over.

Hunter S. Thompson

❧ ❧ ❧ ❧

IT IS BETTER TO BE vaguely right than precisely wrong.

H. Wildon Carr

❧ ❧ ❧ ❧

A HAPPY CHILDHOOD is poor preparation for human contacts.

Colette

❧ ❧ ❧ ❧

HUMOR IS EMOTIONAL chaos remembered in tranquility.

James Thurber

⚜ ⚜ ⚜ ⚜

YOU NEVER REALLY LEARN much from hearing yourself talk.

George Clooney

⚜ ⚜ ⚜ ⚜

IT TOOK ME 15 YEARS to discover I had no talent for writing, but I couldn't give it up because by that time I was too famous.

Robert Benchley

⚜ ⚜ ⚜ ⚜

IT'S PRETTY HARD to be efficient without being obnoxious.

Kin Hubbard

⚜ ⚜ ⚜ ⚜

CULTURE IS AN INSTRUMENT wielded by professors to manufacture professors, who when their turn comes, will manufacture professors.

Simone Weil

⚜ ⚜ ⚜ ⚜

EVERYONE HAS A TALENT. What is rare is the courage to follow the talent to the dark places where it leads.

Erica Jong

⚜ ⚜ ⚜ ⚜

THE VICTOR belongs to the spoils.

F. Scott Fitzgerald

⚜ ⚜ ⚜ ⚜

THE EXPANSION of the universe spreads everything out, but gravity tries to pull it all back together again. Our destiny depends on which force will win.

Stephen Hawking

⚜ ⚜ ⚜ ⚜

GREATNESS IS A ZIGZAG streak of lightning in the brain.

Herbert Asquith

⚜ ⚜ ⚜ ⚜

DEALS ARE MY ART FORM. Other people paint beautifully on canvas or write wonderful poetry. I like making deals, preferably big deals. That's how I get my kicks.

Donald Trump

⚜ ⚜ ⚜ ⚜

A DOG, I have always said, is prose; a cat is a poem.

Jean Burden

⚜ ⚜ ⚜ ⚜

WE DO NOT REMEMBER DAYS, we remember moments.

Cesare Pavese

⚜ ⚜ ⚜ ⚜

ALL TRUTHS ARE EASY to understand once they are discovered; the point is to discover them.

Galileo Galilei

❧ ❧ ❧ ❧

A BOOK MUST BE the ax for the frozen sea within us.

Franz Kafka

❧ ❧ ❧ ❧

THE DREAMER CAN KNOW no truth, not even about his dream, except by awaking out of it.

George Santayana

❧ ❧ ❧ ❧

IT IS A FEELING that no matter what the ideas or conduct of others, there is a unique rightness and beauty to life which can be shared in openness, in wind and sunlight, with a fellow human being who believes in the same basic principles.

Sylvia Plath

❧ ❧ ❧ ❧

THE BOTTOM LINE is in heaven.

Edwin H. Land

❧ ❧ ❧ ❧

A BEAUTIFUL SOUL has no other merit than its existence.

Friedrich von Schiller

❧ ❧ ❧ ❧

THERE ARE NO RULES of architecture for a castle in the clouds.

G. K. Chesterton

⚜ ⚜ ⚜ ⚜

BIGOTRY TRIES TO KEEP truth safe in its hand with a grip that kills it.

Rabindranath Tagore

⚜ ⚜ ⚜ ⚜

DRINKING WHEN WE ARE NOT thirsty and making love all year round, madam; that is all there is to distinguish us from other animals.

Pierre-Augustin Caron de Beaumarchais

⚜ ⚜ ⚜ ⚜

TO DO JUST THE OPPOSITE is also a form of imitation.

Georg Christoph Lichtenberg

⚜ ⚜ ⚜ ⚜

THERE'S NOTHING WRONG with sobriety in moderation.

John Ciardi

⚜ ⚜ ⚜ ⚜

A PESSIMIST IS ONE who makes difficulties of his opportunities and an optimist is one who makes opportunities of his difficulties.

Harry S. Truman

⚜ ⚜ ⚜ ⚜

WITHOUT JUSTICE courage is weak.

Benjamin Franklin

⚜ ⚜ ⚜ ⚜

THE YEARS THAT are gone seem like dreams—if one might go on sleeping and dreaming—but to wake up and find—oh! well! Perhaps it is better to wake up after all, even to suffer, rather than to remain a dupe to illusions all one's life.

Kate Chopin

⚜ ⚜ ⚜ ⚜

HE HAD DECIDED to live forever or die in the attempt.

Joseph Heller

⚜ ⚜ ⚜ ⚜

CONVICTIONS ARE MORE dangerous enemies of truth than lies.

Friedrich Nietzsche

⚜ ⚜ ⚜ ⚜

STOP WORRYING—no one gets out of this world alive!

Clive James

⚜ ⚜ ⚜ ⚜

I NEVER LOSE SIGHT of the fact that just being is fun.

Katharine Hepburn

⚜ ⚜ ⚜ ⚜

ANYONE CAN DO any amount of work, provided it isn't the work he's supposed to be doing at that moment.

Robert Benchley

❧ ❧ ❧ ❧

ALWAYS FORGIVE your enemies—nothing annoys them so much.

Oscar Wilde

❧ ❧ ❧ ❧

THAT IS WHAT LEARNING IS. You suddenly understand something you've understood all your life, but in a new way.

Doris Lessing

❧ ❧ ❧ ❧

A PHYSICIST IS an atom's way of knowing about atoms.

George Wald

❧ ❧ ❧ ❧

YOU MAY HAVE TO FIGHT a battle more than once to win it.

Margaret Thatcher

❧ ❧ ❧ ❧

A POET'S WORK: To name the unnamable, to point at frauds, to take sides, start arguments, shape the world, and stop it from going to sleep.

Salman Rushdie

❧ ❧ ❧ ❧

LEADERSHIP IS A POTENT combination of strategy and character. But if you must be without one, be without the strategy.

Norman Schwarzkopf

🙟 🙟 🙟 🙟

MISTAKES ARE PART of the dues one pays for a full life.

Sophia Loren

🙟 🙟 🙟 🙟

WE LIVE IN A SOCIETY exquisitely dependent on science and technology in which hardly anyone knows anything about science and technology.

Carl Sagan

🙟 🙟 🙟 🙟

ART DOES NOT REPRODUCE the visible; rather, it makes visible.

Paul Klee

🙟 🙟 🙟 🙟

EVERYONE HAS HIS BURDEN. What counts is how you carry it.

Merle Miller

🙟 🙟 🙟 🙟

IF I CAN DREAM, I can act; and if I can act, I can become.

Poh Yu Khing

🙟 🙟 🙟 🙟

ONCE A NEW TECHNOLOGY rolls over you, if you're not part of the steamroller, you're part of the road.

Stewart Brand

⚜ ⚜ ⚜ ⚜

THE HISTORY OF LIBERTY has largely been the history of observance of procedural safeguards.

Felix Frankfurter

⚜ ⚜ ⚜ ⚜

YOU DON'T GET TO CHOOSE how you are going to die. Or when. You can only decide how you're going to live. Now.

Joan Baez

⚜ ⚜ ⚜ ⚜

GOVERNMENT EXPANDS to absorb revenue—and then some.

Tom Wicker

⚜ ⚜ ⚜ ⚜

RESOLVE, THEN, THAT on this very ground, with small flags waving and tinny blasts on tiny trumpets, we shall meet the enemy, and not only may he be ours, he may be us.

Walt Kelly

⚜ ⚜ ⚜ ⚜

AS LEAVES ON THE TREES, such is the life of man.

Homer

⚜ ⚜ ⚜ ⚜

WHAT IS THE HARDEST task in the world? To think.

Ralph Waldo Emerson

❖ ❖ ❖ ❖

ALL THE WEALTH on this earth, all the wealth under the earth and all the wealth in the universe is like a mosquito's wing compared to the wealth we will receive in the hereafter. Life on earth is only a preparation for the eternal home, which is far more important than the short pleasures that seduce us here.

Muhammad Ali

❖ ❖ ❖ ❖

WE DON'T KNOW who we are until we see what we can do.

Martha Grimes

❖ ❖ ❖ ❖

LIFE IS ONE long process of getting tired.

Samuel Butler

❖ ❖ ❖ ❖

IF YOU UNDERSTOOD everything I said, you'd be me.

Miles Davis

❖ ❖ ❖ ❖

NOW the swinging bridge
Is quieted with creepers
Like our tendrilled life.

Matsuo Basho

❖ ❖ ❖ ❖

THE REAL QUESTION is not whether machines think, but whether men do.

B. F. Skinner

❧ ❧ ❧ ❧

A WOMAN HAS GOT to love a bad man once or twice in her life, to be thankful for a good one.

Marjorie Rawlings

❧ ❧ ❧ ❧

ART IS A STEP from what is obvious and well-known toward what is arcane and concealed.

Kahlil Gibran

❧ ❧ ❧ ❧

WORDS ARE MEN'S daughters, but God's sons are things.

Samuel Madden

❧ ❧ ❧ ❧

I'M THE ONE that's got to die when it's time for me to die, so let me live my life the way I want to.

Jimi Hendrix

❧ ❧ ❧ ❧

IF YOU LET PEOPLE follow their feelings, they will be able to do good. This is what is meant by saying that human nature is good.

Mencius

❧ ❧ ❧ ❧

DOUBT ISN'T THE OPPOSITE of faith; it is an element of faith.

Paul Tillich

❦ ❦ ❦ ❦

THERE'S ONE THING worse than being alone: wishing you were.

Bob Steele

❦ ❦ ❦ ❦

AN INJURY IS MUCH sooner forgotten than an insult.

Philip Dormer Stanhope (Lord Chesterfield)

❦ ❦ ❦ ❦

LIFE IS EITHER A DARING adventure or nothing. To keep our faces toward change and behave like free spirits in the presence of fate is strength undefeatable.

Helen Keller

❦ ❦ ❦ ❦

DOGMA IS THE SACRIFICE of wisdom to consistency.

Lewis Perelman

❦ ❦ ❦ ❦

WHEN SPIDER WEBS UNITE, they can tie up a lion.

Ethiopian proverb

❦ ❦ ❦ ❦

THERE SEEMS NO PLAN because it is all plan; there seems no centre because it is all centre.

C. S. Lewis

❧ ❧ ❧ ❧

WE SHALL NOT grow wiser before we learn that much that we have done was very foolish.

F. A. Hayek

❧ ❧ ❧ ❧

THERE ARE ONLY two families in the world . . . the haves and the have-nots.

Miguel de Cervantes

❧ ❧ ❧ ❧

MAN'S CAPACITY for justice makes democracy possible; but man's inclination to injustice makes democracy necessary.

Reinhold Niebuhr

❧ ❧ ❧ ❧

I LIKE MEN to behave like men—strong and childish.

Françoise Sagan

❧ ❧ ❧ ❧

IT IS ALWAYS THE BEST policy to tell the truth, unless, of course, you are an exceptionally good liar.

Jerome K. Jerome

❧ ❧ ❧ ❧

NEVER MISTAKE motion for action.

Ernest Hemingway

❧ ❧ ❧ ❧

THE COURSE OF HISTORY shows that as a government grows, liberty decreases.

Thomas Jefferson

❧ ❧ ❧ ❧

NO SOONER ARE WE SUPPLIED with every thing that nature can demand, than we sit down to contrive artificial appetites.

Samuel Johnson

❧ ❧ ❧ ❧

I WENT TO THE WOODS because I wished to live deliberately, to front only the essential facts of life, and see if I could not learn what it had to teach, and not, when I came to die, discover that I had not lived.

Henry David Thoreau

❧ ❧ ❧ ❧

HUMOR IS JUST another defense against the universe.

Mel Brooks

❧ ❧ ❧ ❧

MUSIC IS THE TIMELESS experience of constant change.

Jerry Garcia

❧ ❧ ❧ ❧

THE KEY TO IMMORTALITY is first living a life worth remembering.

St. Augustine

❧ ❧ ❧ ❧

NO HUMAN BEING can really understand another, and no one can arrange another's happiness.

Graham Greene

❧ ❧ ❧ ❧

BE KIND AND CONSIDERATE with your criticism.... Always remember that it's just as hard to write a bad book as it is to write a good book.

Malcolm Cowley

❧ ❧ ❧ ❧

HE WHO KNOWS only his own side of the case, knows little of that.

John Stuart Mill

❧ ❧ ❧ ❧

SATIRE IS MORAL OUTRAGE transformed into comic art.

Philip Roth

❧ ❧ ❧ ❧

I FIND THAT A GREAT PART of the information I have was acquired by looking up something and finding something else on the way.

Franklin P. Adams

❧ ❧ ❧ ❧

THE WORST, THE LEAST curable hatred is that which has super-seded deep love.

Euripides

❧ ❧ ❧ ❧

WHEN A STUPID MAN is doing something he is ashamed of, he always declares that it is his duty.

George Bernard Shaw

❧ ❧ ❧ ❧

COMMON SENSE and a sense of humor are the same thing, moving at different speeds. A sense of humor is just common sense, dancing.

William James

❧ ❧ ❧ ❧

OH WHO CAN TELL the range of joy or see the bounds of beauty?

Sara Teasdale

❧ ❧ ❧ ❧

THE THOUGHTS WE CHOOSE to act upon define us to others, the ones we do not, define us to ourselves.

Yahia Lababidi

❧ ❧ ❧ ❧

HOWEVER BEAUTIFUL the strategy, you should occasionally look at the results.

Winston Churchill

❧ ❧ ❧ ❧

IF YOU THINK you can think about a thing inextricably attached to something else without thinking of the thing which it is attached to, then you have a legal mind.

Thomas Reed Powell

⚜ ⚜ ⚜ ⚜

WHAT WAS ONCE thought can never be unthought.

Friedrich Durrenmatt

⚜ ⚜ ⚜ ⚜

EVERYONE IS A GENIUS at least once a year. The real geniuses simply have their bright ideas closer together.

Georg Christoph Lichtenberg

⚜ ⚜ ⚜ ⚜

I HAVE A TERRIBLE MEMORY: I never forget a thing.

Edith Konecky

⚜ ⚜ ⚜ ⚜

TAKE WHAT YOU CAN use and let the rest go by.

Ken Kesey

⚜ ⚜ ⚜ ⚜

IF WE WOULD LEARN what the human race really is at bottom, we need only observe it at election times.

Mark Twain

⚜ ⚜ ⚜ ⚜

HOPE is a waking dream.

Aristotle

❧ ❧ ❧ ❧

GREAT THINGS are done when men and mountains meet;
This is not done by jostling in the street.

William Blake

❧ ❧ ❧ ❧

IT IS AT THE MOVIES that the only absolutely modern mystery
is celebrated.

André Breton

❧ ❧ ❧ ❧

I AM A TEMPORARY enclosure for a temporary purpose; that
served, and my skull and teeth, my idiosyncrasy and desire will
disperse, I believe, like the timbers of a booth after a fair.

H. G. Wells

❧ ❧ ❧ ❧

HE'S A MUDDLE-HEADED FOOL, with frequent lucid intervals.

Miguel de Cervantes

❧ ❧ ❧ ❧

IN NATURE, nothing can be given, all things are sold.

Ralph Waldo Emerson

❧ ❧ ❧ ❧

WE ARE MORE OFTEN treacherous through weakness than through calculation.

François de La Rochefoucauld

🙢 🙢 🙢 🙢

THERE ARE BUT TWO POWERS in the world, the sword and the mind. In the long run, the sword is always beaten by the mind.

Napoléon Bonaparte

🙢 🙢 🙢 🙢

SOME BOOKS ARE to be tasted, others to be swallowed, and some few to be chewed and digested.

Francis Bacon

🙢 🙢 🙢 🙢

I HATE TO ADVOCATE DRUGS, alcohol, violence, or insanity to anyone, but they've always worked for me.

Hunter S. Thompson

🙢 🙢 🙢 🙢

A CULT IS A RELIGION with no political power.

Tom Wolfe

🙢 🙢 🙢 🙢

WHEN WE QUARREL, how we wish we had been blameless.

Ralph Waldo Emerson

🙢 🙢 🙢 🙢

NOTHING GIVES one person so great advantage over another as to remain always cool and unruffled under all circumstances.

Thomas Jefferson

❧ ❧ ❧ ❧

MOST HUMAN BEINGS have an almost infinite capacity for taking things for granted.

Aldous Huxley

❧ ❧ ❧ ❧

A NARCISSIST is someone better looking than you are.

Gore Vidal

❧ ❧ ❧ ❧

ONE MAN'S WAYS may be as good as another's, but we all like our own best.

Jane Austen

❧ ❧ ❧ ❧

I'LL TELL YOU A BIG SECRET, my friend. Don't wait for the Last Judgment. It takes place every day.

Albert Camus

❧ ❧ ❧ ❧

FAME IS ONLY GOOD for one thing—they will cash your check in a small town.

Truman Capote

❧ ❧ ❧ ❧

WHEN I WAS YOUNG, I thought money was the most important thing in life. Now that I'm old—I know it is.

Oscar Wilde

⚜ ⚜ ⚜ ⚜

I LOVE MANKIND—it's people I can't stand.

Charles Schulz

⚜ ⚜ ⚜ ⚜

A DREAM IS A MICROSCOPE through which we look at the hidden occurrences in our soul.

Erich Fromm

⚜ ⚜ ⚜ ⚜

HEREIN LIES THE TRAGEDY of the age: not that men are poor, not that men are wicked, but that men know so little of men.

W.E.B. DuBois

⚜ ⚜ ⚜ ⚜

OUR SCIENTIFIC POWER has outrun our spiritual power. We have guided missiles and misguided men.

Dr. Martin Luther King, Jr.

⚜ ⚜ ⚜ ⚜

MANKIND MUST put an end to war or war will put an end to mankind.

John F. Kennedy

⚜ ⚜ ⚜ ⚜

THERE IS A WEIRD POWER in a spoken word.... And a word carries far—very far—deals destruction through time as the bullets go flying through space.

Joseph Conrad

❖ ❖ ❖ ❖

TRUTH IS THE CRY of all, but the game of few.

George Berkeley

❖ ❖ ❖ ❖

YOUTH IS WHEN YOU BLAME your troubles on your parents; maturity is when you learn that everything is the fault of the younger generation.

Bertolt Brecht

❖ ❖ ❖ ❖

LIFE IS THE ART of drawing without an eraser.

John W. Gardner

❖ ❖ ❖ ❖

EVERY TIME I PAINT a portrait I lose a friend.

John Singer Sargent

❖ ❖ ❖ ❖

THERE IS NOTHING more dangerous to the formation of a prose style than the endeavor to make it poetic.

J. Middleton Murry

❖ ❖ ❖ ❖

MEN AT FORTY
Learn to close softly
The doors to rooms they will not be
Coming back to.

Donald Justice

❧ ❧ ❧ ❧

AS SOON AS THERE is language, generality has entered the scene.

Jacques Derrida

❧ ❧ ❧ ❧

SATIRE is tragedy plus time.

Lenny Bruce

❧ ❧ ❧ ❧

THE ARTIST'S TECHNIQUE, no matter how brilliant it is, should never obscure his vision.

Aaron Douglas

❧ ❧ ❧ ❧

I'M AFRAID THAT some times
you'll play lonely games too.
Games you can't win
'cause you'll play against you.

Dr. Seuss

❧ ❧ ❧ ❧

WHAT SANE PERSON could live in this world and not be crazy?

Ursula K. Le Guin

❧ ❧ ❧ ❧

WHEN YOU BREAK the great laws, you do not get liberty; you do not even get anarchy. You get the small laws.

G. K. Chesterton

❧ ❧ ❧ ❧

WE ARE GOING TO DIE, and that makes us the lucky ones. Most people are never going to die because they are never going to be born.

Richard Dawkins

❧ ❧ ❧ ❧

DEATH AND TAXES and childbirth! There's never any convenient time for any of them!

Margaret Mitchell

❧ ❧ ❧ ❧

EITHER GET BUSY living or get busy dying.

Stephen King

❧ ❧ ❧ ❧

DAD TAUGHT ME everything I know. Unfortunately, he didn't teach me everything he knows.

Al Unser, Jr.

❧ ❧ ❧ ❧

I AM NOT YOUNG enough to know everything.

Oscar Wilde

❧ ❧ ❧ ❧

IN THE DEPTH OF WINTER I finally learned that within me there lay an invincible summer.

Albert Camus

❧ ❧ ❧ ❧

I PASS WITH RELIEF from the tossing sea of Cause and Theory to the firm ground of Result and Fact.

Winston Churchill

❧ ❧ ❧ ❧

WHY NOT SEIZE the pleasure at once?—How often is happiness destroyed by preparation, foolish preparation!

Jane Austen

❧ ❧ ❧ ❧

I'M TIRED OF ALL this nonsense about beauty being only skin-deep. That's deep enough. What do you want—an adorable pancreas?

Jean Kerr

❧ ❧ ❧ ❧

GOOD THINGS, when short, are twice as good.

Baltasar Gracian

❧ ❧ ❧ ❧

THERE'S A BIT OF MAGIC in everything, and some loss to even things out.

Lou Reed

❧ ❧ ❧ ❧

THE LESS GOVERNMENT we have the better—the fewer laws, and the less confided power.

Ralph Waldo Emerson

❧ ❧ ❧ ❧

THINK OF THE BEAUTY still left around you and be happy.

Anne Frank

❧ ❧ ❧ ❧

SOME PEOPLE SAY that I must be a terrible person, but it's not true. I have the heart of a young boy in a jar on my desk.

Stephen King

❧ ❧ ❧ ❧

IT IS AMAZING HOW complete is the delusion that beauty is goodness.

Leo Tolstoy

❧ ❧ ❧ ❧

THE FORMULA FOR SUCCESS is simple: Practice and concentration, then more practice and more concentration.

Babe Didrikson Zaharias

❧ ❧ ❧ ❧

WE ARE THE FACILITATORS of our own creative evolution.

Bill Hicks

❧ ❧ ❧ ❧

WE WAKE, IF WE EVER wake at all, to mystery, rumors of death, beauty, violence.... "Seem like we're just set down here," a woman said to me recently, "and don't nobody know why."

Annie Dillard

❧ ❧ ❧ ❧

TOMORROW is our permanent address.

E. E. Cummings

❧ ❧ ❧ ❧

OUR SPECIES NEEDS, and deserves, a citizenry with minds wide awake and a basic understanding of how the world works.

Carl Sagan

❧ ❧ ❧ ❧

AND NOW HERE is my secret, a very simple secret: It is only with the heart that one can see rightly, what is essential is invisible to the eye.

Antoine de Saint-Exupéry

❧ ❧ ❧ ❧

LIFE ISN'T ABOUT FINDING yourself. Life is about creating yourself.

George Bernard Shaw

❧ ❧ ❧ ❧

THAT IS HAPPINESS: to be dissolved into something complete and great.

Willa Cather

❧ ❧ ❧ ❧

SOURCE INDEX

SOURCE INDEX

SUBJECT INDEX

A

Abilities, 287, 320
Achievement, 228, 288, 303, 316, 317, 320, 343, 345
Acting, 68, 144, 146, 302, 338
Action, 14, 37, 271, 296, 337, 357
Activism, 31, 32, 36, 71, 89, 139, 142, 178, 191, 193, 216, 258, 261, 294, 295, 307, 314, 324
Addiction, 197
Advantages, 130
Advertising, 51, 53, 70, 74, 328
Advice, 26, 166, 297, 321
Aging, 11, 14, 24, 26, 28, 31, 51, 60, 73, 77, 112, 113, 120, 131, 148, 203, 207, 245, 246, 249, 250, 258, 259, 269, 273, 293, 308
Ambition, 325
Anger, 28, 103, 116, 149, 150, 180, 185, 197, 273
Animals, 144. *See also* Cats; Dogs.
Anxiety, 75, 131
Appearances, 79
Art, architecture, 28, 32, 34, 35, 41, 55, 67, 85, 97, 107, 109, 113, 116, 123, 124, 128, 130, 155, 160, 166, 174, 177, 180, 206, 207, 210, 223, 244, 251, 259, 263, 281, 290, 323, 330, 333, 336, 341, 348, 351, 354, 365, 366
Attitude, 112, 132, 204, 273
Awe, 13

B

Beauty, 19, 72, 95, 171, 217, 282, 310, 314, 368, 369
Beginnings, 311

Beliefs, 32, 44, 62, 93, 125, 146, 147, 167, 234, 267, 285, 340, 347
Bigotry, 348
Blame, 79, 182
Books, 47, 63, 99, 188, 189, 202, 219, 284, 286, 347, 362
Boredom, 47, 91, 111, 179, 255
Brevity, 368
Buildings, 155, 277
Bureaucracy, 180, 239
Business, 85, 162, 215, 252, 308, 325, 346

C

Calmness, 363
Capitalism, 294
Cats, 212, 270, 277, 321, 239, 346
Celebrities, 231
Certainty, 295, 368
Change, 9, 88, 90, 92, 107, 117, 216, 268, 298, 299, 305, 329
Character, 10, 13, 15, 24, 29, 57, 58, 70, 80, 87, 89, 123, 155, 217, 236, 292, 302, 332
Charity, 176
Charm, 92, 142
Children, 224, 226, 233, 250, 258, 354
Choices, 56, 211
Civilization, 12, 16, 38, 40, 118, 135, 245, 247, 271
Committees, 102, 249, 303
Common sense, 125, 162, 215, 359
Communication, 40, 92, 195, 353
Communism, 183
Compassion, 95, 257, 343
Competition, 134
Compromise, 318
Confidence, 242, 298
Conflict, 220, 362

Conscience, 39, 60, 74, 81, 121, 190, 288
Consequences, 122, 149, 205, 211, 231, 359
Consistency, 9, 34, 339, 355
Control, 39
Conviction, 254, 306, 349
Correctness, 344
Courage, 6, 43, 61, 73, 74, 116, 134, 153, 169, 188, 239, 243, 276, 328
Courtesy, 75, 76, 80, 140, 169
Creativity, 40, 48, 215, 268, 274, 369
Crime, 71, 78, 121, 161, 190, 198
Criticism, 98, 323, 326, 327, 358
Crutches, 265, 319
Cynicism, 105, 144, 186, 333

D

Dance, 199, 312, 315, 330
Death, 14, 20, 33, 41, 44, 83, 86, 96, 97, 100, 101, 114, 165, 180, 206, 213, 222, 234, 236, 242, 258, 302, 327
Debt, 325
Deception, 102, 117, 328
Decisions, 270
Defeat, 292, 313
Delusion, 282, 319, 338
Democracy, 77, 78, 133, 161, 207, 277, 333, 340, 356
Depravity, 290
Desires, 132, 247, 342, 357
Difficulties, 161, 292
Dignity, 120
Diplomacy, 101
Direction. *See* Goals.
Disappointment, 126
Discovery, 262, 319, 330
Discretion, 308